Instagram Marketing and Advertising for Small Business Owners in 2019

The 5 Step Insta-Profit Formula to Create a Winning Social Media Strategy, Grow Your Brand and Get Real World Results

Mark Warner

Dear reader,

As

an independent author, and one man/woman operation - my marketing budget is next to zero.

As such, the

only

way I can get my books in-front of valued customers if with reviews.

Unfortunately,
I'm competing against authors and giant publishing companies with multi-million dollar marketing teams. These behemoths can afford to give away hundreds of free books to boost their ranking and success. Which as much as I'd love to - I simply can't afford to do.

That's
why your honest review will not only be invaluable to me, but also to other readers on Amazon.

Best,

Mark Warner

Table of Contents

CHAPTER 5 STEP 4: INTERACTION, RAVING FANS

CHAPTER 6 STEP 5: TURNING FOLLOWERS INTO PROFIT

CHAPTER 7: INSTAGRAM IN 2019

CHAPTER 8: GETTING AHEAD

CHAPTER 9: CONCLUSION

Chapter 1: Instagram for Your Business

As a small business owner, you have a lot of work on your plate. You have to manage the business, handle clients, solve problems, all the while managing the marketing side of your company. These are complex areas and for the most part, will take up a lot of your time. The last thing most business owners want to do is create *more* work for themselves. And oftentimes, the idea of getting involved with a new social media app seems like just that: more work.

However, marketing is still a major responsibility of the small business owner. Like it or not, you're going to be spending a large chunk of your time working to market and advertise for your products or services. But what if there was a way to streamline your marketing process? What if there were a series of simple steps that could be taken that would increase your profits, build stronger relationships with your customers and promote your brand?

The purpose of this book is to teach you five steps for using Instagram for business success. While Instagram might appear at first glance as a little more than a social media tool for taking pictures of food, the truth is that Instagram is a powerful engine for direct marketing. By learning how to use it properly, you will be able to greatly increase your income while simultaneously decreasing the amount of time you need to spend on marketing.

The Insta-Profit Formula is based on two underlying principles:

1. The key to successful marketing is by creating relationships and telling stories.
2. Your time is extremely valuable.

We won't waste your time with endless amounts of theoreticals and hypotheticals. Rather, we're here to show you proven methods that will get real world results. By following and holding to these five steps, you'll be able to achieve tremendous success using Instagram. And best of all, you won't have to commit hours upon hours a week to achieve these results. You'll learn all the best ways to maximize your marketing results!

So, let's break down exactly what Instagram is and how it's relevant for today's small businesses. Instagram is a social media app owned by Facebook. It primarily focuses on visual mediums, i.e. photographs instead of plain text. Over 500 million Instagram accounts are active on a daily basis worldwide. Who are these users? For the most part, Instagram users tend to be young. 64% of users are between the ages of 18-34. On top of that, those under the age of 25 tend to spend upwards to an hour and a half using Instagram *every day!*

Instagram is also a highly global platform. 80% of its total userbase is located outside of the United States. But don't let that number fool you into thinking the U.S. has a small number of users. It's estimated that there are 105 million Instagram users in America alone! It's a busy platform with plenty of traffic.

In terms of gender demographics, more women use Instagram then men, however, when it comes to daily active users, they are fairly close together, with 50.3% of the userbase being female. The fact that there is little difference in gender makeup means the platform is essentially unisex, making it appropriate for any product regardless of gender demographic.

So, there are quite a bit of people who use Instagram regularly. The question then is, what type of content are they interested in? And does a small business have the ability to reach those users? As for content, it really goes across the board. Users enjoy following a wide variety of different types of accounts and generally move towards accounts that post related to their interests. After all, Instagram is a form of social media. This means that people will aggregate towards their chosen niches and look for a steady stream of content that is related to that niche.

On the business end, however, the numbers are quite impressive. There are currently over 8 million business accounts set up on Instagram.

80% of users follow at least one business account. And on top of that, 60% of Instagram users report that they first heard about a product or service on Instagram. 30% of users even make purchasing decisions based on Instagram posts that they've come across featuring a product.

These numbers show that there is a big market of people who are readily engaging with the platform on a daily basis *and* are willing to engage with business accounts. Ad revenue is staggeringly high on Instagram, in fact, in 2018, they sold over 6.8 billion in ads. This means that advertisers have clearly seen value in using Instagram as a marketing tool and have put out quite a bit of money in order to get their ads in front of the relevant audience.

As you can see, Instagram is a big field, ripe for those who are looking to market their products and services. Let's move on to the first step, where we will learn how to create a customer persona to better help with targeted marketing.

Chapter 2: Step 1: It's all about them

The customer is the most important part of Instagram marketing. If you want to find financial success, then you're going to have to develop a customer first mindset. In everything that you do on Instagram, you must be thinking purely about the benefit of the customer. In other words, it's all about them!

A lot of times, social media marketing can tend to come off as self-serving. A marketer will spend a significant amount of time promoting and talking about their brands and products in the hopes of making sales. However, in reality, marketing efforts that are entirely self-focused fail to capture the interest of potential customers. Most of the time, people are turned off by this behavior. Why? Because self-focus in marketing doesn't provide any *value* to the customer.

At the end of the day, everyone is concerned with what brings value to their lives. People engage with the things that they find valuable and ignore the things that they don't. It's as simple as that. When people engage on Instagram, liking, following and commenting, it's because they find value in those posts. They find enough value that they are motivated to engage, follow and pay attention.

So, the trick to learning how to capture the interests of people effectively is to learn what they value. Then, once you've learned what they value, you simply provide those things to them. In turn, they will begin to pay attention to your marketing efforts and over time, will begin to value your business or your products. This creates a bond which will ultimately lead to your customers making more purchases and being more receptive to your marketing efforts.

So, what do people value? On a consumer level, people value *solutions* to their problems. Ultimately, a customer makes a purchasing decision because they perceive that the product will be successful in fixing whatever problem they are currently facing. All products solve problems. The core of good marketing is identifying what problems your target customers are having, then proposing solutions to those problems. This is what captures the attention of a potential customer.

One of the most important steps to Instagram marketing is to develop a proper customer persona, so you can exactly know what problems they are currently facing. When you have a clear profile of their problems, you can then begin to develop solutions to those problems. Let's take a look at a step by step method of developing the Customer Persona.

Customer Persona

The Customer Persona is a collection of thoughts, concerns and interests that your ideal customer would have. By defining a customer persona, you'll be able to develop a concrete Instagram marketing strategy. You'll be able to determine what kind of content would be the best to share as well as what your customers are going to be looking for.

Developing a Customer Persona is fairly simple to do. All you need is to do is use a series of questions to create a "profile." Then, you'll want to keep that profile in mind whenever you're developing your marketing material. And it's important to know that you can have multiple customer personas. Most products appeal to more than one type of group. By developing multiple personas, you'll be able to develop content strategies to reach each group with specific marketing methods.

The questions below should get you thinking about the customer persona. Your ideal customer is going to be primarily based off of the product that you are selling, so you'll most likely need to do a bit of market research to determine things like age and gender demographics.

Question One: What is my customer's age and gender?

Getting age and gender profile is fairly simple, but a necessary component. Age is extremely important when it comes to different types of marketing methods, or even if Instagram is actually for your product. Gender is important because it will influence how you are marketing the product.

Question Two: What are my customer's interests and hobbies?

The key to developing a good relationship with your customers through Instagram is learning what their interests and hobbies are. The more you know about their interests, the more relevant content you'll be able to create. Try to spend time going into as much detail as you can and create a wide pool of interests and hobbies to choose from. This will help you much more when it comes to planning out a content schedule later on.

Question Three: What are my customer's problems?

Your customer will most likely have more than one problem. Your job is to come up with a concrete definition of what those problems are. Once you are able to describe what those problems are adequately, you'll be able to work on developing methods of communicating with your customers about that problem.

Question Four: What solutions are available to my customer?

While your product or services are the most obvious solution, this question is more about determining the competition that is working to vie for your customer's attention. Spend some time looking at the different solutions that are available, so that you can get a pulse on the competition.

Question Five: How would my product benefit my customer?

Here is where you'll work to put together benefits that solve your specific customer's problems. Don't generalize in this section, write answers that only apply to this current customer persona. For example, if you're selling a product that would appeal to three different customer personas, each persona may look at the product in a different light. What would motivate Customer Persona A to make a purchase might not motivate Customer Persona B.

These five questions will help you to develop a great customer persona. But what do you do with this information once you have it? Well, first and foremost, think of the customer persona as a style guide. Whenever you're working on a marketing effort, you will want to be working to impress that customer persona. Try to think of the persona as a concrete person, an individual who would be looking at your marketing efforts.

This type of thinking helps you work on creating content that is valuable to your ideal customer. With the Customer Persona fully developed, you will be on point every single time you develop an ad, create a post or even when commenting. By keeping the Customer Persona in mind, you will be able to create the kind of value that will attract real-life people who are quite similar to your ideal customer. And unlike your Customer Persona, these real people are actually capable of making purchases!

Summary

To summarize this chapter, one of the most important things that you can focus on is your customer relationship. Rather than worry about your own business' needs or desire, you need to pay attention instead what your customers want and then give it to them.

You must also know exactly who your customer is before you can effectively market to them. Without a clear idea of the customer persona, you won't have a clear idea of what kind of content they are going to enjoy. You won't know what motivates them to buy what you are selling.

Creating a customer persona isn't hard to do, but it does take time and effort. You'll need to sit down and answer some key questions in order to create the right kind of persona. You also need to make multiple personas, one for each possible group that your business or products will appeal to. Try to be as specific as you can when defining a persona.

Chapter 3: Step 2: Set Up For the Long Term

Once you have a clear understanding of who your ideal customer is, it's time to begin working on the more practical side of Instagram marketing: Setting up your Business Profile! While it might seem relatively straightforward, there are a few things that you should keep in mind when developing an Instagram profile.

How to Set Up An Instagram Bio

First and foremost, you'll need to make sure that you are creating a separate account from your personal account. It's all well and good to have your own Instagram profile for personal uses, but you will want to keep your professional and personal accounts separate. This is for a few key reasons. The first is that the personal Instagram page is a reflection of you as an individual. A business profile, on the other hand, is a reflection of your company values. If there are people who are interested in the product but can't seem to find the company profile on Instagram, they may end up not getting further involved. They most likely aren't going to be searching for you by your personal name.

The second reason you'll want to set up a business account is that business accounts have access to extremely important metrics for data analysis. This will help you understand how many people are looking at and engaging with your content.

Step One: Download the App

Instagram is an app for your phone, so the first thing you'll need to do is download it, if you haven't already. You can find the app from either the Apple Store or the Google Play Store.

Step Two: Sign Up

When signing up, make sure that you use your business email, not your personal one. This will be helpful just for the purposes of organizing any incoming messages you get later on from Instagram.

Step Three: Convert to a Business Account

Once you're inside the app, you'll need to go to the settings section and convert your newly made account to a Business Account. To do that, you just need to go to the settings by tapping on the gear, then go to Account. Then, select the *Switch to Business Account* option. This will prompt an invitation for you to link your Instagram directly to your Facebook Business Page. It will be helpful to link the two, because it's easier to move people from Instagram to Facebook and vice versa.

Step Four: Add Relevant Information

Once you have set up your Business Account, you'll need to add relevant information. This means filling out your profile, adding the right kind of profile picture and then selecting the right link.

Staying on Brand

Your brand is one of the most precious things when it comes to online marketing. Your entire company is built around the brand identity that you have created for yourself. A brand identity is composed primarily of a combination of message, visuals and specific colors. You must work diligently to make sure that your brand is highly visible on your profile page.

When an Instagram user lands on your page, there is only a short amount of time to make an impression on them. One of the first images that you'll want them to see is your logo. In general, the logo should always be the profile pic. It's where most users tend to look at first and it will stick with them. This will help develop "brand recognition," meaning that the visitors might end up seeing a product of yours later on and will recall having seen the brand before. On top of that, customers who are visiting your Instagram profile so that they can follow you are expecting to see your logo somewhere, as a means of confirming your identity.

The language you use in your profile description should also accurately reflect your own brand. Feel free to use a slogan as a profile descriptor, but make sure that you are clearly conveying your company's identity in the description. A visitor will see the picture first but will then quickly read the profile. Don't be verbose, either. Be quick and punchy with what you have to say about your company. Use humor if it fits your brand.

What Not to Include in A Bio

Generally, you want your bio to provide a quick "snapshot" of your company, its values and what it offers to the consumer. That being said, there are quite a few things that you will want to avoid when creating a bio. The biggest is unprofessionalism. At the end of the day, you are still a company, even if you are the only running the business. People expect businesses to behave just like a business. This means that you should keep your bio professional as possible. Don't ramble, rant or write offensive content. Don't get political and avoid making any kind of inflammatory statements.

What Not to Use as a Profile Pic

When it comes to using a profile pic, you really have two options. The first is using your logo, which is highly recommended. If, for some reason, you don't want to use a logo, then we would suggest that you use a professional photograph of yourself. The photo should be of high quality.

The list of acceptable photo types is fairly short, but the list of things you shouldn't use as a profile is exceptionally long. In general, you shouldn't use anything unprofessional in your profile pic. This includes poorly lit photographs, images that are blurry, offensive or tasteless images and certainly images that are unrelated to your business. The key is professionalism. There are plenty of ways to appear approachable to your customer, but the first impression that they'll want to get is that your business is legitimate. Don't undermine your great company and product with a poorly lit photo of you on a summer vacation. Keep it tight and professional.

Your Link

You'll notice that Instagram gives you the opportunity to create one and only one link on your profile page. This link is extremely important. Unlike other types of social media platforms, Instagram doesn't allow you to create links inside of your posts. This means that while you will be able to post pictures and all sorts of content, you can't create links that will direct consumers to your website. This is extremely limiting, as it means all traffic will essentially remain on Instagram.

You are provided with one link in your profile and that's it. This means that in order for an Instagram post to move a visitor from Instagram to your website, they'll need to visit your profile. And, since you get only the one link, you'll need to choose very carefully what you link your customers to. In general, you'll want to send them to the most relevant place for your business. For the most part, this would be your main website. However, in some cases, if you're pushing one and only one type of product, you may want to direct them straight to a landing page instead.

Don't make the mistake of simply linking the customer to another social media site. While you might have a more active account somewhere else, you're not actively helping your cause by shuffling the customer around from social media to social media. Instead, try to bring them to your main website where they can begin to evaluate your product for the purpose of making a purchase. Remember, all social media sites are tools meant to help sell products. The last thing you want to do is create a maze for your consumers, redirecting them from site to site until *finally* they are able to find what they are looking for.

Summary

One of the most important things to remember about using Instagram for Business is that you aren't representing yourself anymore. Rather, you are going to be representing your entire company. Even if you are the only employee in your company, you will want people to look at your profile and see an upstanding business that is both professional and good looking.

You need to make sure that you have a good brand profile on your customer page, allowing people to know immediately what your business is about when they land on it. Your link should be taking customers to the most important part of your website and you should have all the contact information present so that customers are able to get in touch with you quickly and easily.

Finally, you should also take care to avoid posting personal matters or opinions on your social media account. The Instagram profile should be solely for the purpose of conveying company opinions, brand messages and photos. Leave all of the personal stuff to your personal account and never mix the two up!

Chapter 4: Step 3: Relationship Building

This chapter will be broken up into two sections. The first will be mostly outlining the nature of how relationship building works in broad terms. The second section will be more focused on nuts and bolts, actionable steps that can be taken to increase your Instagram following. But before we can get into the specifics, it's good to take a step back and look at the whole of what it means to use Instagram for the purpose of marketing.

As mentioned before, everything that you do should be about the customer. The goal isn't to gain as many sales as possible, because a sale is a simple transaction. Once a sale is made, it's done. As a marketer, you'll want to be able to go past sales and create a follower, someone who is passionate about your brand and your products.

A customer buys and goes on with their life, but a follower rants and raves about you. A follower engages with you and with others. Followers are enthusiastic about what they love and become mini-representatives. Best of all, you don't have to pay a follower, because their passion comes from a place of love and enthusiasm for your products.

Instagram is unique in that it allows for businesses to connect with their customers on a closer level. A business owner gets the opportunity to get to know their customers intimately, learn what their interests are, what their hopes and dreams compose of. They get to see aspects of their customer's lives through windows. And in turn, your customers can see what your business is about. The things you post, the content you create, can have a profound impact on the way customers view your company.

If the customer perceives that your business' motive is purely for the sake of profit, that you are just interested in generating as many sales as possible, they will most likely keep you at arm's length. Sure, they may be interested in your product, but that's simply because of the problems that your product solves. If it's a really good product, it will most likely speak for itself.

However, just because a customer is satisfied with the product doesn't mean that they will become excited enough to engage with you. If they view your relationship as a primarily transactional thing, then they will simply buy your products when it suits them, but never engage past that. And honestly, if your focus is purely on generating sales, why should they engage? Once they have made the purchase, there is no more room for them. They move on and you continue to sell your wares.

Yet, there are ways to capture a customer's interest, sell them your product and continue to build the relationship, even after you have made the sale. We call this concept engagement. You don't just want to put out products, you want to engage with customers. You don't just want sales, you want customers showing off pictures of their new purchase. You want to engage with them as people, acknowledging them and helping them. The more you engage with a customer, the more of a connection you will form with them. Over time, this connection will lead to a stronger relationship. And, if things go especially well, they may end up becoming more than a customer, they'll become a follower.

This might seem like it's a bunch of extra effort, but the truth is, it's fairly easy to work to create engagement with customers. It's really just a mindset that you need to hold to. When creating posts, when making content, focus on providing a great experience for Instagram users. Care more about what your customer personas want than what you want. Put people first. The more you can integrate this philosophy into your Instagram marketing, the better the chances you'll convert customers into followers.

Don't underestimate the value of word of mouth marketing. Nielsen states that 92% of people take more stock in a friend or family member's recommendation than any other type of advertising. It's one thing for a business to tell you that their product is great, but when a friend of yours recommends the product, then you know it is worth the money. By working to turn customers into brand advocates, simply by caring about them, you'll be generating significantly more sales than if you were to simply focus on promoting your products without much care of what the customer's want or need.

That's the fundamental core of Instagram marketing: you are building relationships. The more advocates and followers that you get, the larger your company will become. The ability to have a whole host of people who will excitedly recommend you via social media increases your growth potential significantly. And best of all, those customers often stay life-long! So not only do you get the benefits of them marketing for you, but you also get the benefit of them buying your new products! As long as you maintain an attitude of putting the customer first, you'll find tremendous success in building relationships. Now, with that philosophy in mind, let's move on to the nuts and bolts of building relationships through Instagram.

Finding Instagram Followers

While we mentioned followers as a concept to be people who are advocates, in this section we're primarily referring to Instagram Users who follow you on your Instagram Account. Followers are a necessary component to Instagram success for a few reasons. The first reason is that when you make a post on Instagram, the post will show up in your follower's feeds. Then, if your followers like or make a comment on your post, their activity will show up in their friend's feed. This basically allows your followers to promote your profile whenever they engage with your account.

This will naturally increase the number of followers that you have, as users may come across one of your posts and like it enough to visit your profile page. When that happens, they'll have an opportunity to see previous posts. If they like what they see, they could even follow you, which will work to draw in more followers in a perfect cycle.

The second reason you want to have a high amount of Instagram followers is for social proof. When people come across a business that has sparked their curiosity, one of the first questions on their mind will be about the legitimacy of that business. The internet can be a sketchy place, with plenty of fraudsters and scammers about and most people are discerning. They want to be able to determine if the business they are looking at is real and trustworthy.

The more followers that you have, the better chance you have of gaining a potential customer's trust. After all, if 3,000 people are all following a business, they are most likely legitimate. But if a business has only a handful of Instagram followers, it's possible the potential customer might not trust you enough to explore further. That's why it's important to work to get as many as followers as possible in the beginning, to at least give people an understanding that you are an established company.

So how do we find Followers to begin with? When you're just starting out, you can generate more followers by simply working on converting your current fanbase to follow you on Instagram. For example, if you have a business that already has a following, you can run a promotion where if a customer follows you on Instagram, they get a special discount. Or, you can simply make an announcement on your home page and heavily encourage people to follow you on Instagram. Contacting friends and family, asking them to follow you is a great way to boost your initial numbers, even if those individuals are outside of your target demographic.

You should also take steps to include your Instagram feed on your home site, so that people who are coming to your site from non-Instagram links are able to see what you have been posting. This will help passively increase the number of followers that you have. But passive generation isn't enough, at least not when you're just starting out.

Another way to build followers is to begin following people on Instagram who match your customer persona. Part of the Instagram etiquette is to follow back, so if you follow someone, they will generally follow you back. This is a great way to actively build up followers, but you need to be careful about a few things. The first is that not everyone will follow back, especially Instagram users who are extremely popular. Large companies, Instagram Influencers and public figures often have a very small list of the people they are following. This is generally because when an account is that large, they don't need to work on generating followers anymore. Their fanbase has already grown to a significant amount and, unless they say something really bad, the numbers will remain fairly steady.

So, don't waste your time or energy on following major Instagram users in the hopes that they will follow you back. Instead, try to focus on following the regular people who use Instagram daily for the purpose of consuming content. The benefits of this are twofold, first you get followers who are actually interested in the content that you are putting out. This means that they are more receptive to hearing your brand message. Second, you have a better chance of active followers actually engaging with your content. Remember, you want to find followers who are liking and commenting, because this increases the likelihood of other people coming across your content.

So how do you find people on Instagram? The easiest way is to simply search for content that is relevant to your customer persona's interests. Then, look at the people who are liking and commenting on those photos and observe their profile. Do they match your customer persona? Are they similar enough to warrant following? If the answer is yes, follow them! Hopefully they'll follow you back.

You should be discerning with who you follow, of course. Make sure that you are following people who are only in your relevant demographic. Having followers is great, but you want to make sure that they are quality followers, who will respond to your marketing efforts. If you're selling hardcore hiking gear, there's no reason to follow accounts that are primarily focusing on the baking scene. Those people most likely won't convert and if they do, it will require a lot of convincing on your end. That is wasted time and energy. It's better to find a warm follower and heat them up than it is to find a frozen follower and thaw them out!

The last way to find Instagram users is to attract them through the Hashtag system. Instagram has a robust search and categorization system known as Hashtags. Hashtags, simply put, are keywords that when placed in an Instagram post, will be added to the search engine. Then, people who are searching for those hashtags will be able to find those posts. This enables a bunch of strangers, all who don't know one another, to share thoughts and ideas quickly between them. For example, if someone posts

#mondayinspiration, they are joining thousands of other people who are all making different posts but with the same hashtag. They might not know one another, but they are all participating in the creation of a searchable, living index.

When you create posts, you will want to use hashtags properly. This will increase your chances of being discovered by other Instagram users who are searching for that hashtag. Your post will appear in the search section and they may end up interacting with it. If that's the case, it may result in you gaining a new follower! Hashtags are extremely potent and can help move a post out of obscurity into popularity rather quickly, especially if a lot of people are interested in searching for content related to that hashtag.

But there are some limitations to hashtags and discovery. If a hashtag is big enough to the point where it shows up in the trending section of Instagram, it is most likely spurring a lot of people to create posts with those hashtags. This, in turn, will create a flood of posts which will crowd out the search feature and could easily result in your posts being overlooked. If there are too many search results attached to a hashtag, you most likely won't be discovered.

The second limitation to hashtags is the fact that in order for a hashtag to be effective, people have to be searching for it. In other words, you cannot just create your own hashtags and wait for it to be discovered. People will not find your hashtags unless they are specifically searching for that phrase. So, until your Instagram account becomes large enough to set trends by getting followers to also post using your hashtag, you'll need to stick to using already established hashtags.

The trick is to find hashtags that are somewhere in the middle in terms of popularity. Too popular of a hashtag and you get lost in the avalanche of search results. Too few and nobody will bother to search for that hashtag. You'll want to find some hashtags that are trending upwards but haven't already hit their peak yet.

Finding Hashtags

Using hashtags is fairly easy to do, all you need to do is type # and then a phrase afterwards. However, the difficulty lies in actually finding the right hashtags to use. As mentioned in the section above, you need to walk a fine line between obscurity and popularity if you want to maximize your results. So how do you go about finding hashtags and determining their popularity?

Fortunately, the process is easier than you might think. Thanks to websites like Hashtagify, you'll be able to type in hashtags and see how they are trending in terms of popularity, what the related hashtags are like, etc. These data points are extremely useful when it comes to planning out posts in the future. With the proper use of hashtags, you can greatly accelerate your Instagram account growth. Each post that you make will have a better chance of being discovered and engaged with. And, the way that Instagram works is that the more engagement a post receives, the higher up it will be in the search results. Success begets success.

The good news about hashtags is that you don't just get one chance. In fact, a post can have anywhere up to 30 hashtags! That means you are free to do research on multiple hashtags and incorporate them into your posting liberally. If you have two or three hashtags that are performing well, you can place them on the same post and watch as they grow! Of course, there is a caveat here. You want to make sure that any hashtag that you use in a post is both relevant and in the right context.

Relevancy matters because of quality control. You don't want to use irrelevant but popular hashtags because it can leave a bad impression with the viewers. For example, if you were to use a popular baking hashtag to attract people to your hiking post, you are accomplishing two things, both negative. The first is that you are bringing in people who are specifically looking for baking related things. Chances are they'll see in the search bar that the post is irrelevant and ignore it. This accomplishes nothing and wastes everyone's time. The second problem is that people who follow you may notice that you're using irrelevant hashtags and may begin to see you as being somewhat dishonest. After all, trying to widen your net with misleading hashtags isn't a particularly ethical thing to do. This can sour your relationship with your current followers.

Context is also highly important when it comes to using hashtags. Not all hashtags are straightforward in their meaning. There are sometimes concepts or ideas that surround why specific hashtags have grown in popularity. If you don't know the context of how a hashtag is being used, you could potentially create posts that are wildly inaccurate or worse, damaging to your company.

One great example of a hashtag gone wrong is when the hashtag #whyistayed began to trend on Twitter. A lot of people began using this hashtag as a means of discussing what kept them trapped in dangerous, abusive relationships. The purpose of the tag was to raise awareness of domestic violence. Yet, the pizza company DiGiorno had no idea that this was the point of the tag. All they saw was the fact that it was trending on Twitter and decided to use it without checking the meaning first. Their gaffe was "#whyistayed You Had Pizza." This, of course, was wildly inappropriate and caused the company to receive a tremendous amount of flack for their tone deafness.

In general, you'll want to do everything in your power to avoid this kind of behavior. Instead, make sure that you are 100% sure of the context behind the tag that you are using. Look at the posts that are using it and keep a note of the context, it's the only way to be certain that you aren't accidentally walking into a dangerous topic.

A Note About Buying Followers

While you are working on expanding and developing your Instagram following, you may end up coming across websites that offer to sell you followers for a rather reasonable fee. These followers, they promise, look completely real and will even fool Instagram's algorithms. These companies are often hoping that businesses purchase hundreds, or even hundreds of thousands of followers, so they offer bulk discounts for their services.

However, it's important to know that purchasing followers from third parties will do absolutely nothing for your business. While some businesses might think that having a huge amount of followers will help improve their online reputation or give people a good first impression of their business, usually the opposite is true. It's fairly easy to tell if the bulk of an Instagram user's followers are real or not, and once you realize that the majority of a following are just bots or junk accounts made by some third party, the conclusion is fairly inevitable: this user paid for followers. This can damage your reputation.

Another problem with purchasing followers is the fact that these followers will not actively engage or interact with you. They will merely take up digital space. As a business you want your followers to be active as possible, interacting with you and each other, so that they can share your content and make purchases. A fake follower does none of that. All a fake follower does is waste your money. Besides, once Instagram's algorithms pick up the trail of these fake followers, they will purge the accounts, leaving you with nothing. If you want to spend money in the pursuit of getting more followers, you would be much better off using Instagram's ad system.

Posting Strategies

Instagram is a content publishing platform first and foremost. While people are enjoying liking and commenting on posts, having discussions about their favorite subjects, the reason they come to Instagram is to look at pictures in a steady stream. The app itself is heavily designed to create a seamless scrolling experience, allowing users to endlessly scroll down through the hundreds upon hundreds of pictures that are available to them.

Capturing attention isn't going to be easy. When you put a post up on Instagram, you will only be a small part of the Instagram user's feed. They'll have other pictures to look at, and, if your content isn't interesting enough, they won't engage with you. The less they engage, the less chance your posts have of showing up in their feed to begin with, so that could create a dangerous downward spiral. Therefore, you must be willing to focus on developing the right content to share with your followers. There are three components to a proper posting strategy: timing, content and frequency. Let's take a look at each one in detail.

Timing

Instagram focused on the chronological order of posts. That means if you put out a post at 5pm and a hundred of your followers are on using Instagram at 5, they'll most likely see your post. This means being timely is of extreme value, as you will want to make sure that your posts are seen during the time that your users are most active.

Figuring out *when* your followers use Instagram the most is the hard part. Depending on your demographic, they may respond more during the daytime or during the night. Fortunately, there are social media tools out there that will help you to learn the patterns of your followers, so you can calculate an ideal posting time. Then, once you have your time, make sure you only post during that time period, to ensure that your posts show up in the maximum number of feeds possible.

Content

Developing content for Instagram is going to be the bulk of the work you'll have to do. In order to stay both interesting and relevant to your followers, you'll need to be putting out a number of posts a week. Without those posts, you won't be able to drive engagement and lead people back towards your link.

There are many different types of content that you can share on Instagram, but they all have one thing in common: they are primarily focused on the visual medium. This means for the most part, you're going to need to either take pictures, or find them online for distribution. But before we get into the visual aspect of Instagram photos, let's talk about the different types of content that are most popular on the platform.

Infographics

Infographics remain, to this day, as one of the most popular types of content that can be shared through Instagram. People are enjoying both the visual and written components blended together, helping them learn about something relevant to their interests.

Behind the Scenes

As a company, you will most likely have a majority of followers who are interested in your business. Some of them might even be loyal customers who are looking for an inside look at your company. Behind the Scenes photos are a great way to both generate excitement about your business, while also rewarding your followers with content unavailable anywhere else.

The best part of behind the scenes photos is that you'll be able to take them candidly throughout the day, without much planning required. This will allow you to organically share what is happening in your business while also providing you with content to frequently post.

Product Photos and Teasers

One great way to generate more buzz about your business is to show off high quality photographs of your products. Or you can even take pictures meant to tease or hint at the nature of the next coming release. This will help to create more awareness of your products that are available, as well as increase the interest level in what is to come.

Team Introductions and Profiles

The biggest advantage that Instagram gives you as a business is the ability to form relationships with your followers. They don't have to see you as simply just some faceless corporate entity, but rather they can see you as a human company, full of regular, normal human beings just like them. This builds up empathy and a sense of connection. A way to help your followers see your company as more than just a sales platform is to use photos of your employees and team in action.

Of course, you'll want to make sure that your team is comfortable with being posted on Instagram. You don't want to end up in awkward situations where you have team members trying to cover up their faces during candid pictures. And in part of respect for privacy, you should never upload pictures of others on social media without their consent.

Customer Photos

While these photos are not necessarily created nor posted by you, having a call to ask customers to share photos of enjoying your product can be very beneficial. Those who respond and post their photos will be advertising for your product organically, and best of all, it will help to foster more loyalty to your company.

Instagram Stories

Instagram stories are a different type of content from other posts. Normally, when you make a post, you can select a picture from your phone's storage and when it's uploaded, it will be on your profile for good. Instagram Stories work on a fundamentally different level. First, Instagram stories only last for 24 hours from the time they are posted. After that, the story is deleted from Instagram forever.

This might seem strange, but it's a way for people to share highly exclusive content for a very short amount of time. Only those who are following your regularly Instagram will be able to access potentially important information through these stories. This rewards people for making an effort to check in to your Instagram Stories each and every day. In turn, this increases the chances of engagement from your followers. It can even add to more advertising opportunities for you as well.

Second, Instagram Stories are designed to be rawer and less polished. When making a story, you're recording a video or taking a picture to be uploaded immediately. You won't be able to upload a highly polished, well rendered photo, instead it will be more of an honest look at whatever you are recording. This is meant to allow people to feel as if they are experiencing the same thing that you are.

Stories grant a tremendous amount of options for businesses to create all sorts of interesting content. Let's take a look at a few different ways that you can use Instagram Stories to get maximum results!

Generate Buzz Through Slow Reveals

Your business may be working on a new product or some kind of special announcement, such as participation at a big event or convention. Rather than simply come out and announce the product or event, you could slowly work towards it. You'll warm up people as you show small snippets and posts throughout your Stories, generating excitement until you are finally ready for the reveal. Instead of just showing everything at once, you slowly build up to it in the hopes of generating enough of a buzz to warrant preorders or event sign ups.

Create Flash Deals

Since Instagram stories only exist for 24 hours before vanishing, you have an opportunity to create what are known as Flash Deals. A flash deal is quick, lasting only for the time that the Instagram story is online. This will aid you in multiple ways. The first and foremost, it will help to increase sales in a product. As long as you are willing to offer a coupon code, a discount or free shipping, you will be able to get some people to finally make the purchasing decision. This will help your bottom line, and if they are new customers, will help move them into following your business long-term.

The second benefit that Flash Deals provide to you is that you'll be able to create an incentive for your followers to check out your Instagram Stories on a regular basis. This will drive higher engagement as they might be waiting for a deal but could get pulled into other content that you have to offer.

Here's an important note about flash deals. While offering them can be a great way to increase sales and drive engagement, you shouldn't offer too many deals in too short a time. The reason behind this is that if customers miss a flash sale, but see another one just a week later, they'll come to the conclusion that these sales are very common. This conclusion will reduce the urgency of the sale and may lead to them not making a purchase at all, confident that they'll be able to buy later.

In general, you don't want to offer Flash Deals more than once or twice a month. You'll need to keep followers on their toes, never sure when you're going to be putting up a flash deal.

Create a Countdown

Instagram Stories have what's known as stickers, allowing you to add different fun, visual elements to your Instagram Story. One sticker, however, allows for you to turn your story into a countdown clock. This will allow you to show customers that something interesting is coming down the pipeline, but they'll have to wait a certain amount of time before hearing the announcement.

On top of displaying a countdown, the followers will have the option to tap on the *follow* button of the countdown clock. Then, when the clock reaches 0, it will send notifications to those who follow the countdown, alerting them that the timer is over. Then, you can post a new story, with the announcement that people have been waiting for.

Countdowns are another invaluable tool for creating excitement about upcoming releases. If you have a wide customer base that is following you on Instagram, countdowns are a great way to reward them for checking out your Stories.

Exclusive Announcements

Another great way to use Instagram Stories is to use them for exclusive announcements, not found anywhere else. By using Instagram as the platform for these announcements you achieve two things simultaneously. First, you are rewarding your followers with exclusive content not found anywhere else. Second, you are encouraging people who aren't following you on Instagram to do so. This can be a great way to pull in new followers, especially if the announcement is of the utmost importance.

Contests

A lot of businesses use Instagram Stories as a way to host contests. These contests are usually some kind of giveaway that requires action on the part of the follower. For example, you can randomly select a customer from a list of people who use a specific hashtag or post a specific type of photograph as stipulated by the contest. This can considerably increase the number of followers that you have, as contests have a way of attracting new blood who are interested in getting something for free.

Of course, you'll want to be careful with the contest that you run. There are a few things to watch out for. First, you don't want the prize to be too generic, or else you risk people from outside of your target market following you in the hopes of winning. Instead, try to make sure that the product you are giving away is a part of the niche you're selling in. You want to attract followers who will eventually *purchase* your products later on. The cost of the free giveaway is just the cost of marketing.

The second thing to keep in mind is that Instagram does have specific rules for running contests. You must adhere to your local government's laws about promotions and giveaways, as well as make sure that "You must not inaccurately tag content or encourage users to inaccurately tag content (example: don't encourage people to tag themselves in photos if they aren't in the photo)" as stipulated by their website.

Frequency of Posts

Now that you've got a general idea of the types of content that is most popular on Instagram, all that's left is the question of how many times should you post in a week? In general, anywhere between one to three posts a day should be fine. Anything more than that and Instagram will begin to suppress those extra posts. Why? Because, Instagram is a business first and foremost. They want to make money off of other businesses by selling ad space. Using Instagram for free, organic reach is entirely possible, up to an extent. However, posting too many times a day will cause your reach to diminish with each extra post. Instead, it's better to only post up to three times a day, in order for your content to reach the maximum number of feeds possible.

Crafting Captions

While it is true that Instagram is primarily a visual medium, that doesn't mean you won't have to write any words out. Below every Instagram picture is space of what's known as the caption. The caption can be quite short or quite long, depending on what you have to say about the matter. Captions are exceptionally useful for giving your followers context, story or insight into your post.

Captions also drive engagement. When a user sees a photo and likes it, their attention is naturally directed towards the caption section, where they will be able to get more insight on the matter. This space allows you to craft an interesting story for them, or even to ask them questions, prompting an opportunity for interaction with your followers.

So, what are some of the best practices when it comes to writing the perfect caption for your Instagram posts? Here are a few tips:

Support the Picture

Your caption should be in support of the picture that you post. This means that if you're showing a picture of say, an employee working on a project, you should be writing about the project they're working on. Tell a short story, help provide more context to the scenario.

Write the Important Stuff First

Instagram allows you to write up to 2,200 characters total in a caption. This lends to allowing you to write quite a big paragraph if you like. And, there's nothing wrong with writing a longer caption, either. However, you should note that only the first 125 characters will show up when people are scrolling through their feed. They will have to interact with the post in order to see the rest of what you have to say.

This means that the first 125 characters should be crafted in a way that will draw the viewer in. You will need to write a catchy hook that is able to pull them in so that they are willing to read the rest of the caption. So, when writing the first two sentences of your caption, try to think of those words as the "title" of your Instagram post. Will your title be able to draw them in to read more?

Things like hashtags should also go at the end of your Instagram post, not the beginning. The placement of hashtags doesn't affect your search ranking, so don't worry about that.

Create A Sense of Excitement

Remember, at the end of the day, you will want these Instagram captions to help motivate your followers to have some kind of experience. Ultimately, you will want to motivate them to make a purchase or engage more with you, so in order to do that, your writing has to convey a sense of excitement. Write with passion, use a strong call to action when appropriate. Don't just give a boring, bland description of what the viewers see, instead try to stimulate their imaginations and get them excited about what you're sharing!

Avoid being too salesy

It is true that you can use Instagram captions as a means of advertising for your products. And you absolutely should make the occasional pitch or mention that a specific product is currently on sale. However, what you absolutely want to avoid is pushing too hard in your captions. As a general rule of thumb, for every ten Instagram posts that you make, two of those should be geared towards advertising directly. Any more than that and people will start to get the sense that the only thing your business cares about is selling products to them. Any less than that and you won't be able to convert any of your followers into customers!

Get the Point

While you can write a very lengthy paragraph if you so please, remember that people's attention spans are rather short. Everything else on Instagram is vying for their attention, and if you end up rambling too much in your post, they'll just go look at something else. There's nothing wrong with a long post, as long as your writing is both tight and focused. Get to the point as quickly as you can and then, once you've made your point, don't keep writing.

Each caption should really have only one focus, one topic. Trying to stuff too many topics into a single post can not only be overwhelming for the reader, but it can also affect the "punchiness" of your own writing. If you want to write about multiple subjects, make multiple Instagram posts. Don't try to put it all in one overstuffed post.

What to Avoid Posting

Before we conclude this section, let's talk a bit about the things that you'll want to avoid posting when using Instagram for your business. For the most part, you'll want to make sure that you are only posting high quality, good looking images. Blurry and poorly lit snapshots from your phone won't look particularly good and worst of all, may end up causing people to unfollow. After all, people come to Instagram to be wowed and impressed with the visual content in their feeds. An ugly photo could be a major turn off for some.

On top of quality control, you should also work to avoid posting anything *outside* of your target market's interests. You should be laser focused, every post should be as relevant as possible to your customer persona. Any posts outside of those interests will only weaken your marketing efforts.

And last, when posting on Instagram, you should absolutely avoid any kind of controversial, political or inflammatory stances. While making a statement about some popular subject in the news might seem like a good idea, the fact is, people will take both sides of the argument. The last thing you want to do is end up alienating or irritating half of your follower base, just because you wanted to make an important statement. By staying politically neutral, you won't end up risking losing followers (and business) from either side. It's a best practice, especially in today's politically charged environment.

Summary

The best way to build a following through Instagram is to work on creating relationships. In order to create a relationship, you must be more concerned with providing value to your customers than for them to provide value to you. Building a proper relationship requires you to look at them as people and to honestly care about your customer.

Interacting and engaging with your followers on Instagram will help turn them into advocates for your brand. By paying more attention to their desires and giving them assistance when they need it, you are naturally creating advocates who will advertise on your behalf without any prompting.

The best way to gain followers through Instagram is to follow people that match your customer persona. Instagram etiquette dictates that they follow you back, allowing you to build your following over time. Make sure that you only follow the people who are relevant to your company, however, as you don't want to simply build a collection of followers. You want high quality ones who will eventually convert and purchase your products.

Hashtags are some of the most effective ways that you can classify and sort data on Instagram. Through the use of Hashtags, you'll be able to find ideas to plan content as well as help other people who aren't familiar with your businesses to find you. Doing the proper research on hashtags is necessary and you must make sure that you are fully aware of what hashtag actually means before you use it.

Content matters significantly more than most people initially realize when it comes to Instagram. You need to be aware of the kind of content that your followers want to see and then make a point to produce as much of it as you can. Always be innovating when it comes to making new content and most of all, make sure that you aren't coming across as too salesy. The last thing followers want to see is a constant barrage of Instagram salesmen, trying their hardest to make a sale when people just want something to entertain or inspire them.

Chapter 5 Step 4: Interaction, Raving Fans

Once you have a general handle on the type of content that you will be releasing on a regular basis, it's time to take the focus onto the most important part of Instagram: interaction. While posting is extremely important, the truth is, posting is only a means to an end. The end goal of social media is to help move fans closer to you, so that they are able to engage more. The more engagement you get, the better chance you have of gaining their trust and later on, their company loyalty.

It's good to have fans, but as we've mentioned before, what you really want are raving fans. You want people who are so excited about your company and your brand that they are willing to go out and tell other people about it. You want the kinds of fans who will, unsolicited by you, advertise for your products without expecting anything in return.

And with a social media platform like Instagram, it is totally possible to work towards creating those types of fans. Note, that you don't really *find* those types of fans, rather, you actually work to create them by cultivating a strong, healthy relationship with them. Over time, those normal fans will develop into advocates for you. However, this requires that you be significantly more focused on your customers than your own company at first.

Remember, people are ultimately concerned with themselves first. It's all about the customer, not you. So, in order to get stronger fans, you're going to need to develop a content strategy that primarily focuses on increasing connection with your fans as well as driving engagement. This whole section will be dedicated to helping you learn different methods of increasing customer engagement, while simultaneously building more brand awareness in your followers.

Using Comments Properly

If you want to develop relationships through Instagram, you're going to need to spend time on the comments section of not only your posts, but also the posts of other. It's all well and good to make as many posts as you like, but if you aren't commenting, you won't be able to have that personal interaction with others. The proper commenting procedure will enable you to not only maintain an online presence, but also to move people towards your own Instagram profile page passively.

The first thing to keep in mind when commenting on other people's posts is that you want to keep your focus entirely on them. Feel free to praise their photo, talk about what you like about it, etc. However, you should definitely *not* try and move the conversation over to talking about you. You don't want to come across as simply spamming your own information inside of other people's comments. Instead, work to make a genuine effort in communicating with users.

In general, when interacting with others, you're going to want one of three things. You'll want to either encourage, inquire or solve a problem. Encouragement is easy enough, you just keep a positive, healthy attitude and spread love to others. Inquiring is really about asking the user a question or follow-up question about their post. Something to prompt the other person to engage in a dialogue with you and maybe even with others.

However, most likely the bulk your comment work will be geared towards solving problems, often through answering questions. When you see a person in the comments ask a question that you know how to answer, you should make an effort to reply to that individual and share what you know. If they are a follower of yours, they will find you to be helpful and friendly, and may be more receptive to your marketing efforts later on. If they aren't followers, your assistance might be able to motivate them towards following you.

Other ways to solve problems is to make recommendations for products, share helpful tips, give insight into what the problem is and, in some cases, even refer to your own products. Try to keep your sales pitches low, but if you are in a situation where you can genuinely help a person who has a problem with your products, you may even want to consider giving them a coupon code, to help them move along with the sale.

Responding to Comments

Posting a comment is a very proactive thing and can be useful for your business as you grow. However, while posting comments is optional, depending on how much time you have, responding to comments on your own post is decidedly less of an option. Why? Because, as a company and a brand, you're going to want to create as much of an appearance of being active and responsive as possible. When people comment on your own posts, they are taking time out of their busy day to make an effort. Whether they are praising your product, asking a question or just talking about their experience, your followers deserve to be replied to. In doing so, you show that you value and care about them. Ignore them and they might not comment on your posts after a while.

Of course, figuring out what to say can be a bit difficult, especially if a follower is just posting a simple, short word of praise to you. The easiest way is to just reply, short and sweet with a thank you. Other options include using Emojis as quick, easy replies. A heart emoji can go a long way and most businesses do use quick replies like that, so it wouldn't seem out of place.

When it comes to customer concerns or complaints, you should absolutely work to respond to those comments as fast as possible. However, it is important to remember that your conversation is not private when it comes to comments, everyone else can see the exchange. So, no matter what, you'll need to be both civil and diplomatic with your customer, even if you don't think the complaint is legitimate.

The best way to handle customer service complaints is to try and take the conversation private as quickly as possible. Either suggest that you carry on the conversation on in your direct messages, or request that they email so that you can handle the problem.

Social media is rapidly becoming a way of circumventing the drawn-out process of submitting problems to customer support. People are growing fed up with the fact that they have to submit tickets and then often get some kind of frustrating, automated message back to them. Sometimes they can't have their problems solved by the support team. What customers are finding, however, is that when they begin to complain about their issues on social media, it forces the company to respond quickly, or else they risk having their reputation damaged.

So, don't be surprised that if some of your customers who have problems take to social media such as Instagram to complain about you. They may even end up tagging you, as a hope of catching your attention. It's important here to remember that the reason for this behavior is usually born out of frustration and not maliciousness. Most customers just want their problems solved and when the products they use don't work as advertised, they often want to air their grievances. Taking an adversarial approach to these customers will only cause you more harm in the long run.

Even if a customer is malicious in their words against you, a harsh response will almost always prove to make you look petty and unprofessional. Remember, whatever you post online will stay online indefinitely. Even if you change your mind and take down the post quickly, someone will have already taken a screenshot of it and will distribute the post around the internet channels. That is why you must always keep your cool and stay diplomatic.

Handling Trolls and Moderating Comments

There are really two types of commenters online, people who are genuinely just trying to find solutions and interesting content and then there are trolls. The fact that one can be anonymous online combined with the fact that there are no repercussions for abusive or nasty actions has lent to creating a larger pool of people with nothing better to do than to harass and cajole others online. These people, trolls really, get a big kick out of causing trouble and making others suffer.

Part of working with Instagram is learning how to determine whether a commenter has legitimate complains and frustrations, or whether they are just trolling, trying to get a reaction out of you. A legitimate customer is usually looking for some kind of resolution, and while they may be upset or angry, you can generally calm them down once you are able to address the issue at hand. However, with a troll, you will quickly find that they will just say whatever it takes to get a rise out of you. In some cases, they may even devolve into slurs and inflammatory speech that has no place in your posts.

Trolls don't even have to target you, they can very well just put their aim at a follower of yours who posted a comment on one of your photos. If that's the case, you have options for handling these types of people. Thankfully, Instagram does grant you the ability to moderate comments, including putting together a language filter that automatically removes comments that use certain words or phrases.

All you need to do is go to settings and then go to the comments page. This will allow you to create automatic filters that delete posts based on certain words used. There are also manual filters that allow you to place phrases that you want to hide automatically. This is extremely helpful because it automatically moderates your comment sections and prevents the trolls from doing harm to your customer base.

You also have the power to delete someone else's comments on your own posts if you so choose. All you need to do is swipe right on their comment and you'll be given the option to delete it. This can be useful for when someone is clearly being inflammatory or a troll, but they aren't using slurs or phrases that would be picked up by the automatic filter. The cleaner you can keep the comment sections, the better!

However, you must be cautious when moderating the community that you are building around your Instagram profile. The ability to delete anyone's comment can be very alluring, especially if you see a customer make a negative comment about your product or customer service. However, in doing this, you are no longer simply working to preserve the peace, you are instead actively censoring your customer base so that you make yourself look good.

There are some serious problems behind this kind of behavior. The first and foremost is that it will signal to the customer who is complaining that you genuinely do not care about them nor their complaint. This will tell them that your company isn't worth trusting and that you would rather look good than admit fault. You will most likely lose that customer for life. And besides, nothing stops that customer from making their own posts talking about your censorship.

The second problem is that if your behavior gets caught by the community, trust will rapidly diminish. The fact that a company is willing to actively censor and delete comments from people who aren't giving them glowing reviews is extremely shady. You don't want to risk losing your good reputation simply because you chose to remove a few bad reviews. It's just not worth it.

Addressing Criticism

So, if censorship is the worst possible thing you can do when a customer is criticizing your business online, what is the best option? Ultimately, you'll need to determine if there is validity to that criticism. If there is, apologize for their pains. This is an act of humility, but in doing so, you are demonstrating to the customer that they are more important than you. Then, once you apologize, take steps to make it up to them. This effort can turn even the most frustrated customer into an advocate for your company. It's one thing for a company to provide a good service or product, people generally come to expect that. However, when a company is willing to admit error and take steps to make things right, that is above and beyond what most people are expecting.

What do you do when the criticism isn't valid? Perhaps the customer's expectations weren't properly aligned or maybe their complaint is just kind of nitpicky? Just try to address their concerns without talking down to them. When people are having a problem, most of the time they just want to feel *heard*. Validating a customer by listening and responding, being as helpful as possible can go a long way. You don't have to apologize for something that your company isn't responsible for, but you should at least show the customer that you care and are paying attention. You'll find that most of the time, the customer will be happy with your response. Sometimes, a customer will still be frustrated or make negative comments, but after you try to resolve it amicably, just stop responding. Some people will never be happy.

The Snark Trend

Recently, thanks to some aggressive snarkiness from the Wendy's Twitter account, companies are beginning to treat certain critics with a degree of attitude. Some make wry, snarky comments that mock the poster, while others are absolutely ruthless in their treatment of the customer. This creates a bit of fun for followers, as they get to see these normally reserved companies suddenly act out of character towards their customer base. A lot of times, these snarky replies become viral and end up being circulated around on various social media platform.

Being from the outside, it is easy to see the allure of using witty comebacks against negative commenters. First off, it's fun to watch and secondly, it allows you to give others their just desserts, especially if their negativity is uncalled for. But you should be cautious when considering whether to be snarky and dismissive towards commenters.

Most of the time, the companies that are so cleverly dismissing naysayers are quite large in size. Wendy's, for example, is a gigantic franchise that sprawls across the United States. They sell millions of burgers a year and most of their customer base doesn't come from social media. So, in a sense, they have the luxury to behave as they wish. Sure, there is potential for backlash, but Wendy's is large enough to where they can absorb the risk of such backlash. People are going to be stopping at Wendy's regardless of what they say on Twitter.

However, as a small business, you don't have the same luxury. When using your own Instagram account, you will most likely be advertising to people who aren't familiar with your brand at all. Many times, your Instagram posts will be the first point of contact for potentially new customers. Their perception of you matters greatly. While you may believe that you're throwing out clever zingers at negative individuals, if a joke falls flat, or worse, looks like bullying, you could end up losing a lot of good will from your follower base.

So, while snarkiness has begun to trend on social media among the bigger companies, the question you'll need to ask yourself is if you can handle the backlash. If you lose even just one sale from a comeback gone wrong, is it worth it? Tread carefully, you don't want to take one step forward and then three steps back, just because you want to emulate what these multi-million dollar companies are doing.

Increasing Engagement

Engagement has tremendous value for your Instagram posts. First, it increases the likelihood that others will see your post. Second, engagement also increases the chances of a customer connecting more to your brand. The more familiar a customer is with your company, the better chances you have of converting them to a sale.

All of the above posts are really about how to engage properly on your end. Moderating comments, handling critics and answering questions are all great ways for *you* to engage with your followers. But now, we must bring attention to the question of how to drive your followers to engage more. Ultimately, you want every post you make to have plenty of likes and lots of comments. But how do you get there? There are a few different factors involved with engagement. Let's take a look at each one.

Relevance

Once you have a clearly developed customer persona, you'll need to focus completely on uploading posts that are relevant to your customer base's interests. Posting outside of those interests won't net you the results that you're looking for, and worse yet, may even end up hindering you. Remember, you have to anticipate the content that your customer *wants* and then distribute it for them. The more relevant and enjoyable quality content that you can distribute, the more engagement you will naturally get. This should really be the baseline for driving engagement. Put out what the people want and then watch them engage with it.

Popularity

Relevance alone, however, doesn't determine if a post will perform well. In reality, you don't really know how a type of post is going to do until you put it out there. It's possible that content that you think will do really well ends up getting no love while other posts that you didn't think would perform end up generating the most likes and comments.

You can use this information to determine what the best content is to release on your platform. Take a look at the elements of the most popular posts and do your best to try and replicate them. You may find that these posts continue to perform well, generating the most amount of likes and comments. If that's the case, you should continue focusing on releasing more content similar to the successful ones. Don't worry about the posts that fail to perform, instead, try to emulate the ones that are the most successful. Over time, this strategy will help you continually get more and more engagement from your followers.

Remember, it doesn't matter what content that *you* think is good. It's all about the customer's choices and tastes. If they don't like the type of post that you make, no matter how much you personally enjoy it, you have to stop making those kinds of posts. Go only towards what resonates with your followers. Leave everything else behind.

Asking Questions

As mentioned before, asking questions is one of the key methods of getting engagement from your followers. Creating posts that ask simple questions like "what's your favorite thing to do in the morning" or product specific ones like "what's your favorite color of our product," will by default, lead your more interested followers in engaging with you.

But you need to find the right kind of balance when it comes to asking questions of your audience. You can't simply put out dozens of generic posts that ask questions. Too many questions in too short a timeframe will most likely end up being ignored by your viewers. Instead, try to ask one or two questions a week, but make them interesting enough to where the viewers will want to engage with you. This takes time to figure out, of course, as you'll need to ask questions that are relevant to your audience and capable of provoking intelligent discussion.

There are things to steer clear of, when asking questions. First and foremost, you'll want to avoid the types of questions that are overly sales oriented, especially if you have a small customer base. Questions like "what product are you most excited about buying," can be a little too much, as it assumes the customers are planning purchases.

In general, asking questions should be relegated to getting consumers to share their own thoughts and opinions, not as excuses to sell them on your products. You want to spark conversations that will get other people involved. A good, productive question will spark dozens if not hundreds of comments and will further your goals of increasing the overall range of your posts.

Another thing to avoid is any subject that could potentially become inflammatory. As we've mentioned already, things like politics and current events have a tendency to set people off and the last thing you want is to have a comment section full of people whose comments have been deleted by the filter. You should also pay attention to the attitudes towards specific subjects in the niche you've selected. If you know there are certain strong opinions about one style vs another, then you should steer clear of asking people which they prefer.

Polls and Quizzes

A great and interactive form of asking questions on Instagram is to create polls or quizzes that ask what users prefer. Creating them is fairly simple to do as well, all you need to do is use Instagram Stories and then use the appropriate stickers to set these polls up. Generally, you can create two option polls that will let users select between two ideas. You'll be able to see how many users voted for option A and for option B.

Polls are a great way to not only get people to engage in simple preference questions, but also to get a snapshot of what your customers find interesting about your products. Here, you'll be able to ask questions about what type of products or features that your customers would be most interested in. While it's not the most scientific method of data collecting, you'll still be able to get a snapshot of what your customers will be most excited about when it comes to making a new release.

Quizzes can increase the "fun" factor of a page as well. Asking silly, odd or even offbeat questions can provoke all sorts of great answers from the audience. People will see those answers in other feeds and perhaps even be motivated to answer the questions themselves.

Price Temperatures

There are plenty of barriers when it comes to making a purchase decision. One of the biggest can be the price point of the products you are selling. If you are in a niche, or a field that doesn't have a tremendous amount of competition, you will be free to set prices however you like. But, if your prices are too high, you may end up discouraging customers from making purchases. It can be difficult to tell what your customers are thinking when it comes to making these purchasing decisions and even with all the metrics in the world, it can be a bit of a guessing game.

Fortunately, you can just simply ask your followers directly questions about pricing. You can't make it terribly obvious that you're planning on adjusting the price to whatever the customers want, or else they'll just throw out the lowest number possible. But you can ask questions about theoretical deals or short-term sales and see if they respond. If you get overwhelmingly positive results from a question about dropping a price down a few bucks, or creating a bundle deal that will increase savings, then you are taking the guesswork out of pricing!

Summary

If you want to have fans that are more than just followers, but advocates who follow you closely, you're going to need to put in both the time and the effort through engagement. Engaging with an Instagram follower means that you're willing to reply to their comments, like their posts and ask questions that provoke more discussion from your followers.

Not everyone on Instagram is an upstanding citizen who wishes you well. There are plenty of trolls online who only want to cause problems for both you and your followers. You should take time to build a language filter and enforce it on your posts, preventing trolls from using hateful speech and slurs against other commenters. You should work diligently to make sure that the comment sections are safe, free of personal attacks and calls for violence. There's nothing wrong with deleting comments of others that are inflammatory.

However, censorship is not the appropriate course of action when it comes to dealing with people who are legitimately criticizing your actions or your company. Rather, you should work to make things right with those individuals, trying your best to repair the relationship so that they walk away happy.

Asking questions and creating polls are a great way to get people to open up and begin a dialogue. The more you get people talking about the things they like, what they enjoy about their own lives, the more opportunities you have to learn about your customers. This will help you later on when it comes to creating or marketing new products.

Chapter 6 Step 5: Turning Followers into Profit

Using Instagram Ads for Increasing Followers and Engagement

Organic reach through Instagram is great but has its limits. While it is possible for you to build up a follower base through only free, organic use of Instagram, the truth is that it will take quite a long time to do so. As you've seen in the above sections, there are a lot of details involved with putting together a successful Instagram profile and running it does require a bit of a time commitment. As you keep at it and become more adept at using Instagram, you'll find that the time requirements grow less and less demanding, but at the beginning, if you're just using Instagram without paying for ads, you're paying with another currency: time.

Yes, Instagram is technically free and yes, you can technically grow your page nice and large without spending a dime. But that doesn't mean you aren't losing money. Your time is just as valuable as a dollar, more so if you consider that you can be using your time to generate more income for the business. Like with anything else, you have to learn how to calculate opportunity cost. The allure of free can be strong, but if Instagram takes 8 hours a week of your time, you have to be willing to determine what else you could be using that time for. If those 8 hours could have been used to earn your business say, $500 in income, perhaps by making cold calls, then those 8 hours of Instagram weren't free. They actually ended up costing you $500 in profit that could have been made.

One mistake that many business owners make, especially when they first get started with using Social Media is to see the low, low price tag of "free" and assume that they won't have to spend a lot of money in marketing. The truth is, organic, free reach through Instagram is like using sticks to light a fire. It will work, eventually, and only after some serious effort. Paid advertising, on the other hand, is like using a flamethrower to get a fire going.

Overall, the cost of using paid Instagram Advertising is significantly lower than the cost of doing it all yourself for free. You're going to get better results with Instagram Ads than you are with just using your own methods. Why is that? Simply put, because Instagram Ads use Facebook's targeting algorithms.

As individuals use Instagram and Facebook, the system itself is busy learning what the user likes exactly. It learns their behaviors by tracking their actions, the time they spend on specific content and most importantly, it learns to predict which behaviors the user will engage in. Then, using this data, they will place ads in front of people who are most likely to react positively to that ad. In other words, Instagram's targeting algorithms are entirely designed to put your ads in front of people who will most likely follow, engage or even make a purchase!

Instagram ads allow you to target the exact customer persona and then place your promoted posts in front of them. They are then free to engage with your post, either by liking it or even following your page. This will boost your numbers considerably. Best of all, since you're paying for the ad space, these posts are guaranteed to go in front of Instagram users. You don't have to worry about your post not showing up in other feeds, it is a guaranteed if you pay for it.

Ultimately, the benefits of using Instagram Ads drastically outweigh the drawbacks. Even if you have a relatively modest advertising budget, you can still bring in a lot more followers using these ads as opposed to just going the free route. Because not only can you gain more post likes, you can also directly promote links to specific websites, as the one link rule only applies to unpaid Instagram profiles. You are free to create an ad for a specific product, run it on Instagram Ads and then link people to that product's landing page.

This means that over time, you will be able to build a direct link between how much you're spending on Instagram ads and how many sales you are getting from them. Eventually, you'll be able to calculate the cost of customer acquisition, which will then give you a key insight in how much it will cost your business in advertising before you are able to make a sale.

Those kinds of tools just can't be found outside of paid advertising. You may be wondering, if paid advertising is so powerful, then why bother with any of the advice found in the rest of this book? Wouldn't it just be more effective to only pay for ads and not bother about creating good content and building relationships? Not at all!

While paid ads are extremely potent for acquiring new customers and helping people become aware of your brand, that is only one half of the equation. The acquisition might lead to a one-time sale, but maintaining a relationship is what helps lead to more and more sales in the long term. A regular social media presence will ensure that those who have converted and are fans of your product and company, will still be able to interact with you and see what you're up to. More importantly, you'll be able to passively advertise to them on a daily basis.

So, there is a purpose of having both a paid advertising focus as well as having an organic marketing focus. The two together will achieve different goals. One will bring in more customers and increase your sales, while the other will help you keep the business of old customers, periodically reminding them of your products. With that in mind, let's go ahead and get into the specifics of how to make the most of using Instagram Ads in 2019.

Ad Campaign Goals

Running an ad on Instagram is easy to do. All you need is to pick a campaign goal, an appropriate picture or post and then find the target audience. The campaign goal is what determines how Instagram is going to be running your ad, how much it will cost per click and more importantly, what the end goal of the ad is going to be. You have a few options to select from, let's go over them quickly.

Brand Awareness

This option is primarily geared towards Instagram profiles that are trying to get more people aware of their business. If you're going to promote a post, for the purpose of simply making people aware that your product exists, without having an explicit call for action or next step for the customer to take, this would be the right one to use. Why use the Brand Awareness option? Because you can get significantly higher levels of reach with it. While it's not explicitly calling for customers to take action, it helps increase brand recall. Brand recall is important when advertising later down the road, mainly because a customer who recalls your brand from previous ads has a higher chance of engaging. Think of a brand awareness campaign like planting seeds that you will reap later. Get the idea in their mind at first, warm the customer up and then later on, reap the rewards with a direct ad campaign.

Reach

Reach is similar to brand awareness, but with one big difference. The reach goal is simply focused on maximizing the number of people who see your ad. Brand Awareness tends to focus on finding people who are the most relevant before showing them the ad. Reach instead looks to just get your ad out in front of as many people as possible, sacrificing some of that specificity. However, if the products you are selling aren't targeted and the general population would benefit from it, Reach is a great way to help potential customers become aware of its existence.

Traffic

Traffic is a consideration goal, meaning that you're actually aiming for more than just generating brand awareness. The traffic option means that you are looking to put your Instagram ads in front of people who are going to have the highest probability of clicking on the ad and visiting your website. This, of course, can lead to higher levels of sales if you're directing them to a specific sales page. However, you can also use this traffic goal to direct potential consumers to things like your website's blog or event page as well.

Engagement

If you're looking for page likes, comments and follows, then you're going to want to use the Engagement option. The Engagement goal essentially searches for and targets individuals who are most likely to respond to your content. Usually this response is either liking or commenting on your post. You can use the engagement goal when you're looking to increase the amount of feedback on a single type of post of yours.

App Installs

If your business sells an app or has a custom app built for helping customers place orders, you can pitch the app directly to Instagram users with this option. Best of all, when the customer selects this option, they will be transferred to their phone's app store with the option to quickly download your app. This can be a great way of getting more downloads without making your users go through a bunch of hoops in order to find your app.

Video Views

If you have a video on your Instagram, you may want to consider using video views to promote them, especially if the video is a product announcement.

Instagram Story Ads

When users are browsing through Instagram stories, swiping through the various people that they follow, sometimes there are ads in between these stories. These Story ads are often short, quick and punchy. Most importantly, Instagram Story ads are unavoidable. While the other types of ads that you can run on Instagram can just be scrolled past quickly, an Instagram story user has no other option than to wait for the ad to run its course before they can move on to the next story.

This means that when you run an Instagram Story Ad, you have a captive audience for a short time. You can use Story Ads to directly sell to your target demographic, essentially running a mini-commercial for them to enjoy. However, just because you have their attention for a short amount of time doesn't necessarily mean that they will be interested in the products you are presenting. You'll need to work to put together a decent ad, one that will capture their attention past the initial few seconds of realizing they are looking at an advertisement.

Creating a Story Ad is a little different from other Instagram ads, in the sense that these story ads have to be well produced and put together like a min-commercial. You have the option to create either photo ads, video ads or carousel ads that let users scroll through multiple pictures. There are quite a few things involved with putting together a well-made story ad, so let's take some time to review the qualities of what makes for a good story ad.

Attention Grabbing

In general, people don't like ads. Advertisements are just about everywhere, and they tend to be exceptionally invasive in our lives. When we see another ad for the one billionth time that week, we tend to be a little irritated. This puts the advertiser in a negative position automatically, as people are never relieved nor happy to see an ad pop up on their screen. Sure, they might not have any other option than to just let the ad play out, but that doesn't mean they have to pay attention.

You have a very, very short window of opportunity when you display your ad in front of the consumer. You must focus on trying to grab their attention as quickly as possible, through a combination of eye-catching visuals, a clear message and a hook that is interesting.

The hook doesn't need to be anything flashy or crazy, it just needs to spark enough interest to the point that the consumer is willing and ready to continue watching your ad. If you look at most of the successful short advertisements out there, you'll notice that they all have the same effect on people: they draw them in.

A hook doesn't necessarily need to be funny either. Some hooks focus on being mysterious, visually appealing or strange to look at. Some hooks use music or a catchy lyric to draw consumers in. You don't have to create a hook that is against the spirit of whatever product you are selling, you just need to be sure that you have something to pull viewers in.

Storytelling

At the core of advertising is storytelling. People respond to the stories that are being told to them through ads. A good ad incorporates a story of some sort. The story doesn't need to be overly complex, nor does it need to be spelled out, but it does need to be present. Simply saying "buy my product," isn't engaging or interesting. It doesn't hold interest and it certainly doesn't get people to remember your product for later on.

Fun Visuals

Ads don't always need to be garish, but they do need to pop out. Good visuals, a proper blend of colors and enjoyable typesetting will contribute greatly to getting people to pay attention to your ad. Try to stick with colors that pop out at viewers, while also avoiding the drab, boring colors. Of course, you do want to stay within the perimeters of whatever product you are selling, if you're selling business products to professional companies, you might want to stick to more neutral, inoffensive colors as opposed to if you were selling to a surfer crowd.

A Call to Action

It's all well and good to tell people about your product, but if you don't have a call to action that moves them forward, you are essentially wasting your ad money. You need to have a clear call to action that conveys both urgency and opportunity. Consider using phrases that urge the user to commit action, such as "buy now," "on sale for a limited time," or "only while supplies last." These phrases can help a user make a faster decision, especially if they see the value of what they are gaining. Feel free to include discounts or special deals that would get them to make the proper decision, this will only strengthen your call to action and move them through the sales process faster.

Music

Music works well with advertising for two reasons. The first is that music creates and conveys specific moods, feelings or emotions. We, as humans, resound with certain types of music and can be greatly affected by it. Look at any serious, somber or beautiful ad, chances are, if you remove the music it's not nearly as serious or somber. Music allows you to set the tone that you want your customers to experience when they see your ad.

The second reason music works well with advertising is the fact that music creates association. People often remember little songs or sounds from what they've heard in the day and sometimes it can get stuck in their head. If they're humming a tune from your ads, chances are they might remember your ad too.

Most Instagram users actually browse Instagram Stories with their sound on, which leads to a perfect opportunity for you to include music in your ad. In order to play music, however, you will need the commercial rights to that song. The best way to go about finding music to play on your ads is to look for royalty free music that doesn't charge per use. You only pay a single time, flat fee to use the music and then you don't have to worry about paying royalties to the artiest.

Fortunately, the process of finding royalty free music has become greatly streamlined. There are plenty of websites out there that sell licenses to use those songs commercially. You just need to make sure that you check the copyright information, to determine whether you are able to use the song multiple times, whether you're required to credit the artist, etc. However, the process of acquiring royalty free music has become much more streamlined in the recent years and you should have little trouble finding music that goes along with the feeling you're trying to convey with your ad.

Putting it All Together

Combining music, visual appeal, good story and tightly written copy will help to make an excellent story ad. Take your time when creating your ad, don't rush through the process. Customers won't be able to find your ad again, once it's out of their vision, it's gone for good. So, you have to make the right impression on them, or else you risk being forgotten. Take your time, develop a killer looking ad and then watch how well it performs!

Creating Shoppable Posts

If your company primarily focuses on selling physical goods, then you might have an option to create what's known as Shoppable Posts. Shoppable posts are like regular posts, except they display products and also show a price point, allowing for customers to quickly buy your products, using Instagram as the jumping off point.

However, you can't just start creating shoppable posts, due to Instagram's policies. You'll need first to become an approved vendor, which means meeting the requirements that Instagram has for all of its vendors. These requirements, as taken directly from Instagram's support page, are below:

To use shopping on Instagram, your Instagram account and business must fulfill the following requirements:

- **Comply with our merchant agreement and commerce policies.** Your business complies with our merchant agreement and commerce policies

- **Have an Instagram business account.**
  Your Instagram account must be converted into a business account.

- **Have a connected Facebook Page.**
  Your Instagram business profile must be connected to a Facebook Page. Facebook Pages with the Message to Buy payment option will need to delete and create a new Shop with another payment option before they can use shopping on Instagram. Please note that country or age restrictions on your Facebook Page will not carry over to your Instagram account.

- **Primarily sell physical goods.**
  Your Instagram account must be a business that primarily sells physical goods. We are continuing to test this feature and hope to expand availability to more accounts in the near future.

- **Have your business account connected to a Facebook Catalog.**
  Your business account must be connected to a Facebook catalog. This can be created and managed on Catalog Manager or Business Manager on Facebook, or through Shopify or BigCommerce platforms.

These are fairly easy to meet requirements and won't take much of your time. After you've taken these necessary steps to get your account qualified for shoppable posts, you'll need to go to the Business section of the Instagram Settings page on your app and then select the Shopping on Instagram button. This will take you through the steps to confirm an application for the ability to make shoppable posts. Once you've finished, you'll receive a notification from Instagram if you were approved.

Shoppable posts are highly useful when you want to create interesting, fun pictures that feature your products. Since you have the ability to highlight and tag specific images with a name and a price tag, you don't have to create a photo that only focuses on the product.

Finding Your Audience

As we've talked about extensively in this book, a keen awareness and understanding of your customer persona is necessary if you want to be successful in using Instagram for marketing. The data you've collected and put together pays off when it comes to creating ads on Instagram, as you'll be able to create what are known as Audiences.

In advertising terms, Audiences are how Instagram is able to properly target the right demographic to place the ads. An Audience is composed of several different data points that you input when you create your very first Instagram ad. Generally, you'll be giving Instagram all of the information that you've collected, targeting an age group, country, gender makeup and then the interests and behaviors that you are looking to target.

Instagram makes it fairly easy to put together your first audience. As you input the data, you'll see the overall size of the group you are targeting on the righthand side of the page. You'll also be given an estimate as to whether your perimeters are broad or narrow. In general, you want to create audiences that are large enough to where you won't run out of people to advertise to, but not too wide, or else you may end up paying more for ads in the long run. You want to find an audience size that is closer to the middle, where you have room to grow, but the ad space isn't in so much demand that the cost of the ads increases.

Once you've created your first audience and run your first ad, you'll be able to look at the analytics that Instagram provides as to who engaged with your ad, who clicked on it and the general makeup of those who interacted with your ads. We will cover this in a later section, where we will discuss analytics.

You can create multiple audiences. This will help you greatly when it comes to running specific ads that will only appeal to one type of customer persona. For example, if your product appeals to customer persona A, who likes what you sell because it saves them valuable time, but it also appeals to customer persona B, who likes your product because of the price point, you should create two separate audiences, one for each customer persona.

This differentiation will allow you to run two completely different ads, targeting each Persona. You are then free to create one ad, extolling the virtues of how much time is being saved through the use of your product, and then another ad talking about how much of a bargain your product is. You can run the ads simultaneously, targeting two different groups at the same time. This will significantly increase your results than if you were to run just one ad for both groups.

Why is that? Because customer personas might not overlap as much as you would hope. While it would be great to have developed on "uber-persona" that encompasses all of your customers, but you won't be able to market to all of them at once and make it appealing. The more people that you try to please at the same time, the more disappointed they will become.

It's far better to use specificity as a means of capturing the right audience member. It will cost you no more to target only one specific audience at a time, but it will yield better results. The more appealing you can create ads to target one persona at a time, the better off you will be.

Audiences from Lists

If you have an email list that is already functioning, then you're going to want to import those emails into Facebook through the audience section. Those emails are then compiled, and Facebook begins to create a list of people who are similar to the habits and actions of those emails that you have collected. This gives you a big advantage when it comes to finding new customers, as a fully developed customer profile will help Facebook find the perfect people to put your ads in front of.

If you are unfamiliar with an email list, a list is simply a collection of emails that you gather from those who are in your target demographic. Generally, you gain emails from offering special deals or giving away free products. You can then use these emails to send direct advertisements to your customer base, helping move them along closer to converting.

Another term for collecting emails is known as "lead generation." A lead is a person who is relevant to your sales goals, but also interested enough to give you their personal data. A lead can be worth quite a bit of money, because once you have them hooked, you'll be able to continuously market to them at a significantly reduced cost.

There are many ways to build an email list, so we won't go into all of them, but Instagram does offer an option to create a sign-up through their ads. This option is known as Lead Generation in the advertising goals section. Here, you can offer something of value to the Instagram user in exchange for their email.

Ad Pricing

Cost of ads is determined by how many other companies are trying to place ads in the same target market. Each company "bids" against each other, increasing the price of the ad space until the pricing evens out and a final price is determined by whoever has the biggest budget. So, if you're attempting to enter into a demographic that sees a lot of advertisers attempting to buy ads, the price of ads will be higher than if you were to find a niche that had a smaller number of advertisers.

In general, most of the types of ads that you'll run on Instagram will have what's known as cost per click. CPC simply means that you are only charged when an individual clicks on your ad. So, for example, you could run an ad to 1,000 people, but only 100 would actually click on that ad. With CPC, you'll only be charged for the 100 who actually engaged with your ad. This is helpful because it means that you're essentially only paying for the results you're looking for. While you might not be able to guarantee purchase orders or gaining new followers with CPC, you are still only paying for the people who exhibit interest.

Instagram ads run off of a specific budget that you plug in. Say you give them a maximum budget of $20. This means that Instagram will run your ad until it receives $20 worth of clicks. Depending on how crowded the ad market is in that sector, the clicks could be cheap, or they could be expensive. Instagram usually gives projections as to how much engagement or reach you'll receive based on the budget that you give them.

There will be room for experimentation when you're just getting started with running paid ads. There are things you can do to reduce cost, such a tweaking your target audience or finding a new target audience entirely. You'll have to spend time learning what your cost of customer acquisition is, and once that has been finalized, you can work to lower that cost.

Try, Try Again

One of the key principles behind marketing on Instagram is that you will see the best results the more times you run ads. Many small businesses make the mistake of running ads once, seeing no results and then chalking the whole thing up to be a waste of time. The truth is, Instagram advertising allows you to collect valuable metrics and data, giving you the ability to improve the effectiveness of your ads each time you run them.

In other words, it's not a sprint, it's a marathon. You will need to be disciplined to examine what went wrong after you see that an ad returned with very little results. You'll need to be willing to look at the analytics and data to see where you could improve. The more you work with ads, the better you'll get. It's a skillset, just like any other part of being a business owner. You just have to put in the effort and not give up just because there were no initial results. If you stick with it, you will get results through Instagram paid advertising.

Metrics and Analytics

One of the most powerful tools that we have in the advertising arsenal is data collection. When you run ads or even regular posts, Instagram is busy taking note of the behaviors, activities and makeup of the people interacting with your posts. They aggregate this data and put it together for you to be able to study. Metrics and analytics are some of the most important components of running a proper Instagram advertising campaign, because it will allow you to understand the actions that your customers are taking.

Without data, all of your efforts will essentially just be guesses. You need to have a clear understanding of how your ads, your posts and your Stories are performing each month, or else you won't be able to put together an effective strategy for the future. This requires that you spend time looking at the various data points provided by Instagram Insights.

Instagram Insights is your first tool when it comes to data collection. With Insights, you'll be able to see the overall behavior of individuals when it comes to interacting with your Instagram Profile. You'll be able to see how many people have visited your profile, see how many people are clicking on your website as well as what your audience is composed of.

These data points are important because they can help you understand the effectiveness of your actions. For example, let's say that you have a high level of engagement, perhaps your posts are getting an average of 100 likes a day. But your website visits through Instagram are nonexistent. No one is visiting your site. Clearly this is an indicator that something is wrong. It will be on you to determine what is going wrong in this scenario and work to fix it, but without the data collection, you would have no way of knowing whether any of your efforts are working at all.

Basic Metric Types

There are four basic types of metrics to evaluate when looking at Instagram analytics.

- **Reach**: Reach represents how many unique people saw your content. For example, if you had a reach of 100, it means that 100 different users all saw your content throughout the post or ad's run.
- **Impressions**: While reach represents unique views, Impressions simply means views. So, if you had 1,000 impressions in a single day, it means that 500 people could have seen the content twice, or perhaps one person saw it 1,000 times. Impressions are just a general way to gauge how many times your ad or post has been seen. You can combine reach and impressions together to get an idea of not only how popular your content is, but also how many people are coming back to see it again. For example, if you have a reach of 200, but impressions of 500, it means that 200 people viewed your content multiple times. This is a good indicator that your content is resonating with your current viewership. Pay attention to numbers like this, it will help you plan more content for the future
- **Clicks:** This is fairly self-explanatory. With clicks, you are able to tell how many people are clicking on your post links. Generally, you'll only see clicks when looking at the Instagram Ads analytics page, as normal Instagram posts do not allow for linking outside of Instagram
- **Engagement:** Anytime a follower takes a specific action such as liking a page, commenting or replying to a comment, that counts as engagement. Overall, you'll be able to see the engagement rate of your followers and calculate how much they are engaging compared to the number of people viewing your content. Generally, you want to see your engagement rate as high as possible. If you realize that your impressions and reach are quite high, but engagement is suffering, it is very possible that there is something wrong.

There are plenty of other metrics that Instagram has to offer when it comes to advertising. Most of these metrics are extremely specific and can help you determine just how much you have paid for ads, the price per click, what the cost of customer acquisition is and more. However, these data points are only available for those who are actively using Instagram ads. Fortunately, there are other ways for normal Instagram Businesses to gain deeper metrics.

Third Party Metrics

While it is true that Instagram offers quite a bit of metrics and analytical data, they don't always get the entire picture. If you're looking to find a more comprehensive way to analyze data, complete with easy to read reports, assessments and highly accurate pictures of your followers' growth and behavior, then you may want to consider working with a third party metric service. Oftentimes, these third parties allow you to gain access to even deeper, more specific analytics and provide suggestions as to how you can grow even more. The only downside to these services is that they often charge a monthly fee for their services. However, if you are growing considerably, you might want to use a third party that will help keep a bird's eye view on all of the data points you'll need to sift through on a weekly basis.

Instagram Conversion Metrics

After you've run ads on Instagram, you'll want to see how those ads are performing, not just in getting people to click on your ad, but also when it comes to making purchases on your site. The first step in this process is creating what is known as the Facebook Pixel.

The Facebook Pixel is a cookie, or tracker service, that attaches to people who end up on your website after clicking on one of your ads or links. This pixel can be customized to monitor specific actions or behavior on your website, triggering when that action is complete. Then, the information collected by the pixel is reported back to Facebook, and you'll be able to monitor the behavior on their analytics section.

This will allow you to track specific actions performed by your customers. For example, you can set it up so that if someone clicks to purchase a product you are directly selling online, Facebook will track that behavior. This will allow you to learn the actual conversion rate of your Facebook ads. Remember, just because a customer is willing to click on your website link doesn't necessarily mean they will make a purchase. You might be able to guess how effective your ads based on the number of purchases made in correction to the ads you are running, but Facebook pixels allow for you to take the guesswork out of the equation entirely. You will be able to clearly understand not only how effective your ads are in getting a conversion, but you'll also be able to see what pages the average customer visits, how long they stay on the site, etc. All of this data will allow you to determine a more accurate cost of customer acquisition.

Creating a Facebook pixel isn't hard to do. You just need to navigate over to the Pixel section of the Facebook Business Manager area and follow the instructions they provide. After you finish that, you'll just need to follow the steps necessary to create all the events that you want. In general, you will want to make sure that the Pixel triggers every time a customer takes action on your website, such as purchasing a product, emptying their cart or even just clicking on another page. This will help you significantly in the long run.

Retargeting Campaigns

The biggest benefit that the Facebook pixel provides is the ability to do what is known as retargeting. When an individual visits your website, thanks to clicking a link on Instagram, they might be very interested in what you have to sell. They could potentially even be close to converting, but for some reason, they put it off. Perhaps they didn't have enough money to make the purchase immediately, or maybe they just got distracted by something else. The internet is a wide place and there are no shortages of things that are vying for your attention online. It's easy to lose interest in what's in front of you.

Not all interested customers will convert immediately. In fact, it's rarer to get an instant conversion than it is to slowly warm a lead up into making the purchase decision. But just because the client didn't make the purchase doesn't mean they never will. Rather, it means that for some reason they just chose to delay. If you're tracking the behavior of these customers with the help of the Facebook pixel, however, you will be able to run a retargeting campaign, reminding them of the existence of your product.

Retargeting simply means that you are running another ad set in front of a specific group of people, the ones who have clicked on your ad, but didn't convert. Retargeting is a highly effective method of advertising, as these potential customers have already displayed that they are initially interested in your product. All you need to do is run another ad set, perhaps even offering some kind of discount or motivator, retargeting a custom audience.

Building a customer audience using retargeting data is fairly easy to do, all you need is to visit the audience section of Facebook Business Manager and use the data provided by your Pixel. This will create a specific audience, composed entirely out of the people who have visited your website before thanks to your advertising efforts. Of course, you will need to have a large enough group size in order for this to work. If the group size is too small, Instagram won't be able to run the ads, so you'll most likely need to collect data over a larger period of time, or run bigger campaigns before you can retarget.

However, once you have enough of an audience size to run a retargeting campaign, you will see much higher conversion rates than before. Why? Because those who decide to engage with the ad a second time are most likely going to convert, or else they wouldn't have bothered to click on the ad. This can lend to a higher conversion rate as well as cheaper advertising costs. Best of all, it will help you get a better picture of how much effort total it takes to convince a customer to make a purchase.

Summary

Organic advertising is free but is still has a price attached to it: your time. It's much better for you to spend money and get guaranteed results than it is for you to spend hours upon hours of your life trying to get free publicity. Opportunity cost is a real thing and your time also has a cash value, so make sure that you spend it wisely.

Instagram Ads allow you to have unparallel reach through Instagram. You can gain significantly more followers, product sales and even more email sign ups if you are willing to pay Instagram to advertise. Instagram Story Ads are also extremely effective, allowing you to capture the undivided attention of an Instagram user for a few seconds, without giving them the option to simply scroll past your work.

Experimentation is a major part of running ads on Instagram, especially when you're new. It is possible that the first few attempts to make money through Instagram will fail, but that's perfectly normal. It takes time to learn how to master the system and how to hone your advertising efforts so that you make the most amount of money possible.

The data collected thanks to Instagram's advertising system allows for you to calculate your cost of customer acquisition, as well as learn which customer persona is responding the most to your ads. With the help of metrics, not only will you be able to improve your ads, but you will also be able to decrease the amount of money you are spending on ads by learning to retarget customers who are already warmed up to you. By investing your money in a retargeting ad campaign, you will be significantly increasing the chances of getting more sales.

Chapter 7: Instagram in 2019

Technology changes rather quickly. Thanks to the various innovations and changes that happen in the online space, we can never be certain about what is around the corner, especially when it comes to online marketing. The fact is, if you're going to be using social media marketing sites like Instagram, you're going to need to pay attention to trends, statistics and how things are shaping up in the future. Nothing is guaranteed to remain the same, especially since people's tastes can be fickle. What is true today may end up false tomorrow. With that in mind, let's take a look at the trends and snapshots of Instagram user behavior in 2019, as provided by The Preview App.

Photos vs. Videos

According to the statistics, 84 percent of Instagram users are primarily focused on looking at photos as opposed to the mere 15 percent who like to watch videos more. This, of course, should come as no surprise, as Instagram's major claim to fame is based entirely around sharing photos that people like. While it is true that Instagram provides the option to host videos, the fact is those videos aren't getting as much attention as the photos. Why is this? Most likely because there are already better competitors in the video market out there, YouTube.

This isn't to say that you shouldn't make videos, however. If you have a sufficient reason to do so, feel free to create a video, but just don't rely on making too many of them, as that is not the primary reason people are interested in using Instagram right now.

Instagram Story Performance

Instagram stories are growing significantly in the last year. One trend is that more and more people are using Instagram stories for themselves, in fact over 86 percent of Instagram users like to post their own stories. This indicates a strong trend of story content out there, but the question is, how many people are looking at these stories?

Truthfully, according to these statistics, most users still prefer to look at posts than to look at stories. 63 percent of users look at posts more than stories, whereas only 36 percent engage with stories more. This, just like the videos, shouldn't be terribly shocking news. Instagram Stories are still growing, but in general, people still prefer to engage primarily with photos.

What does this mean for your business? It means that if you have only one area to focus on, then photos are your best bet. Instagram stories are helpful means of boosting your popularity with your current fanbase and Instagram story ads can be helpful, but you shouldn't divide your time equally between the two. Over time, it is possible that Instagram stories will become more popular, but for now, photos are still the undisputed king of the medium. Therefore, it of the utmost importance that a significant amount of time is spent creating good photos and visual content to distribute. Stories shouldn't be neglected, of course, but they are just to be treated as supplements to the main event.

Hashtags

While Hashtags might not seem as relevant today as when they were first introduced, the fact is, on Instagram hashtags are still going very strong. Over 59 percent of Instagram users follow specific hashtags, meaning that they will be the first to see when new posts with those tags are released. On top of that, 83.6 percent of Instagram users still use hashtags when making their posts. When it comes to how many hashtags people prefer to use in their posts, there was a split in the results. 39 percent uses less than 15 hashtags, whereas 40 percent prefers to use 15-30 hashtags. The remaining 19 percent uses a total of all 30 hashtags in their posts.

These numbers indicate that, for the most part, hashtags are still primarily used on Instagram with no signs of slowing down. When it comes to the question of how many hashtags to use in a post, it's a mix between 15 to 30. This points to the trend that people aren't really concerned with how many hashtags they are using, just that they are still using them in full force.

Consumer Decisions

When it comes to planning or preparing a purchasing decision, whether it's buying a product, visiting a location for a holiday or even visiting a restaurant, 62 percent of Instagram users say they use Instagram to make those decisions. They use Instagram for finding new places to visit locally, to decide whether they want to buy some new item or if they want to visit a specific store. This is a healthy trend that indicates that the majority of Instagram users look to the platform in the hopes of finding something that will interest them.

However, while it is true that Instagram users are looking to plan their consumer decisions via Instagram, shopping on Instagram is an entirely different story. The majority of Instagram users, 65 percent, has never made a single purchase directly through Instagram. However, this may simply be because Instagram is fairly newer to the scene when it comes to creating things like shoppable posts. As Instagram continues to grow and develop their support for direct sales, we may see these numbers increase considerably.

IGTV

If you're not familiar, Instagram TV, or IGTV, is Facebook's attempt to compete with YouTube. They released the video uploading and streaming service in 2018, as an entirely separate app from Instagram. Their hopes, it would seem, would be to provide a platform for Instagram users who want to expand more into video production. While IGTV is attached to a different app, the program is still being pushed through Instagram, as videos from IGTV can be viewed on Instagram.

The fact that Instagram Videos from IGTV will now be appearing in the feeds of users will undoubtedly increase the number of people who decide to use IGTV, but according to the study, only 17 percent of the IG community is actively using IGTV. The rest are most likely watching the streaming giant that is YouTube, a platform that is showing zero signs of slowing down in size and scope.

So, is IGTV worth it? It's hard to say. Instagram TV is brand new to the market but has been developed by the people who have made both Facebook and Instagram very successful. There is simply no way of knowing right now whether it will be able to compete effectively with YouTube, or to offer a replacement app for the people who want to watch videos through Facebook. But for a small business, it's important to know that IGTV has potential.

IGTV allows for you to upload full length videos, upwards to an hour long. On top of that, the fact that IGTV will also push content to feeds on Instagram means that you have a built-in support network that YouTube cannot offer you. So, if for some reason, you have a need to be releasing long form video content, IGTV might actually be the best platform for you, especially since it synergizes so well with Instagram right now.

Only time will tell whether IGTV will be a success or not, but sometimes there is a tremendous reward in being an early adapter!

Ads

The question on many advertisers minds is whether or not Instagram ads will continue to be relevant in 2019. Will people still be willing to click on ads, despite the sheer rise in the number of ads they encounter on a daily basis? The answer to that question is a resounding yes! According to the study, 81.6 percent of Instagram users click on ads. A number this large is extremely exciting, as it signals that people are becoming more and more accepting of the value that ads do provide to their lives. With such a large amount of people clicking on ads, it means they are finding new and interesting content or products that are compelling enough to get them to interact. This is a good sign for the future!

Image

Another question that the poll asked Instagram users was whether they cared about how many followers an Instagram Profile had. 72 percent stated that they did, in fact, care about how many people were following an Instagram user. The reason for this is most likely because of social proof. An Instagram user who only has a few followers is seen as small, less trustworthy and perhaps even boring. Consequently, a profile with a large number of followers is seen as having already established themselves. When it comes to these types of things, perception can be a reality. If 72 percent of people are concerned with how many followers a profile has, then it would be in your best interest to work towards building enough followers to make you credible!

Time Spent

One of the most important questions that we need to be answered is how much time the average Instagram user spends on Instagram. The answers to this question vary, based on the interests, hobbies and needs of each individual and the poll reflect four different answers. 50 percent of users reported using Instagram for 1 to 3 hours per day. That is about the average makeup of the Instagram user, they tend to use Instagram in the evening, or during downtimes such as lunch.

23 percent of users report using Instagram for only an hour a day, 17 percent admitted to using IG for 3 to 5 hours per day. And 8 percent stated that they used Instagram for more than 5 hours per day.

These numbers are more or less to be expected. There will always be a small portion of the population that overly engages with an app, as well as a portion that underutilizes. But for the majority of users, spending 1 to 3 hours seems reasonable enough.

So, what do these numbers mean for a business? Frankly, you don't have to worry too much about people not seeing your content because they weren't using Instagram. Rather, you need to worry about working with the Instagram algorithm to get it on your side.

Instagram Algorithms in 2019

One of the things that all social media marketers are going to have to contend with is the fact that all social media platforms operate through the use of algorithms. These algorithms can be changed at a moment's notice, to better improve the user experience, or to punish unethical practices that are causing problems for the social media platform itself. You must always make a point to stay on top of understanding how the current algorithm sorts content, how it displays said content and what behaviors it rewards and what behaviors it punishes. These are extremely necessary if you want to stay on the cutting edge of Instagram.

Let's take a look at some of the elements of the Instagram Algorithm that are present in 2019. Fortunately, unlike a few other social media engines that prefer to keep their information about how the algorithms private, Instagram has gone on the record with sharing exactly what their algorithms are looking for when sharing your content to relevant audiences.

Relationship

Instagram's algorithm is able to recognize the interaction between two different profiles, enough so that it can recommend content based on their relationship. For example, if a follower is greatly interacting with you, leaving comments and liking pictures, Instagram will take notice of that. The algorithm will then make a point of providing more of your content to that follower, since they have an established relationship with you.

What this means for a business is that you can't just have your content pop up in a follower's feed just because they follow you. Rather, you need to have some kind of established relationship in order to have your content more frequently show up in front of them. Fortunately, this is not the only factor involved in how Instagram determines where your content shows up.

Interests

As we've stressed greatly throughout this book, relevancy is extremely important, not just so that your followers will get what they are looking for, but also because Instagram wants to put the most relevant content in front of those followers. With the power of photo recognition abilities and machine learning, Instagram is able to look at the actions and behaviors of a user and then predict what kind of content they would like. Then, the algorithm works to make sure that more of the relevant content will arrive on their Instagram feed. If your content is deemed relevant by this algorithm, you have a better chance of your posts showing up in your follower's feeds. If it is not deemed relevant, you will most likely end up passed over in favor of other content.

Frequency Updates

Each time an Instagram user logs in to the app, they will be greeted with content that is the most popular on their feed. However, if an Instagram user likes to log in multiple times per day, there will be a better chance of other, less popular posts showing up in their feed, as Instagram is also focusing greatly on providing new and interesting content to show their user. Therefore, if you target primarily active users who like to use Instagram multiple times per day, you will have a better chance of your content being seen, even if it isn't the first thing shown in their feeds.

Tools to Use in 2019

Instagram itself is a tremendous platform that gives you a wide range of options and tools at your disposal. However, this doesn't mean that Instagram's tools are the end-all, be all of the market. There are a wide variety of specialist programs out there that will help you supercharge your Instagram career, boosting your ability to get results as well as helping you generate more followers and better posts. Let's take a look at a few different tools that remain popular to use in 2019 for businesses using Instagram.

Buffer

Buffer is a social media management app that does it all. It allows you to create posts through Buffer, tracks engagement as well as letting you run multiple social media accounts all from the same platform. The ability to schedule posts ahead of time is extremely valuable, as you can spend a shorter amount of time planning out your posting schedule. Rather than have to manually post multiple times a day and per week, you set one time aside to sit down and plan out all the posts that you want to make. You can put all of your content together in one session and then, schedule what days and times you want those posts to be published. Buffer will do the rest.

The only drawback to using a social media scheduler like Buffer is that it's not free. You will need to pay a monthly fee in order to use their services, but then again, time saved is money saved. Rather than struggling to come up with posts day after day, it's much easier just to sit down once a week and plan it all.

Hashtagify.me

Hashtagify allows you to do proper research on your hashtags. It will not only allow you to find relevant hashtags but will also recommend hashtags based on what you've been searching. This is an invaluable tool for research and planning. On top of that, there is a paid option that allows you to access their library as well as labs, providing you with even more tools to find the best possible hashtags.

Shorby

If you want to have more than one link on your Instagram page, you don't have any options within Instagram itself. However, by using Shorby's services, you can bypass that by adding more links to your Instagram page, taking users to any link you so choose. The downside here, of course, is that Shorby does cost a monthly subscription, but if you are looking to add more links to your Profile page, then this is one of the few ways to do so.

SocialRank

Analytics are extremely important and with SocialRank, you can get some of the deepest insights into not only your audience size and makeup, but also about the audience members themselves. SocialRank works to help you identify your followers, learn more about them and even sort them into categories. This can be highly effective when it comes to learning new customer personas, as you'll be able to look at all of your followers and determine which persona they fall under. You may even end up learning about new personas entirely.

Boomerang

There is a type of Instagram video that seems to be in a constant loop, seamlessly moving back and forth from one action to the other. These are a special type of videos known as boomerangs. You can create these by downloading the boomerang app. It allows you to take ten photos in a burst, then creating a sort of stop-motion effect, allowing you to create a video that moves back and forth, like a boomerang. Boomerang is free to download and easy to use, and the videos can be fun and interesting, especially when you use them for product displays.

What Not To Do On Instagram in 2019

Tastes change, as we've already established. Some practices that worked well in the old days aren't nearly as effective as they are today. And, sometimes there are myths, bad ideas and tips that are circulated by those unaware of the fact that Instagram is constantly changing. Here are a few things to avoid doing in 2019:

Ignoring Influencers

The Instagram Influencer has become one of the most powerful types of marketer in recent years. With the rise of Instagram models and Instagram profiles with hundreds of thousands of followers, advertisers have taken notice of the fact that they can pay Influencers to promote their products organically.

Instagram Influencer marketing has become quite the industry, with many advertising companies finding ways to create links between influencers and business who are looking to expand their market through new and unique advertising methods. Some influencers are taking home enough money to live full time, others are even doing so well that they can go on expensive trips and see the world, all the while sharing their lifestyle with their following.

As an Instagram user, there are two different responses to these influencers that can be bad for your bottom line. The first response is to look at these Influencers, who are certainly doing well for themselves, and come to the conclusion that it would be great if they could help you out somehow. Many times, a smaller profile will attempt to curry the favor of an Influencer, in the hopes of gaining more publicity and attention. This almost always fails, simply because the smaller profile has very little to offer to the Influencer. After all, if an Influencer has 300,000 followers, gets to post Instagram pics all day and gets paid from product sponsorships, why should they have to worry about someone with only 50 followers?

The second response is to look at how great these Influencers are doing and come to the conclusion that they would never be interested in a collaboration of any kind. Or worse, they come to the conclusion that Influencer marketing is all hype and isn't worth caring about.

Neither of these responses is the best approach when thinking about Influencers. If you're willing to make the right efforts, working with an influencer will pay off in spades. As we've talked about before, social proof is one of the most important things in the online economy. When an Influencer, who has a host of fans who adore and care about their opinion, recommends a product, it is almost on the same level as if a close friend had recommended that product. It is significantly more effective than celebrity endorsements and has incredibly high conversion rates, much higher than traditional Instagram ads.

The real difficulty in working an Influencer is figuring out the best method of approach. The first response we talked about, attempting to ride on their coat tails in the hopes of getting some recognition from them, isn't the way to go. Why? Because just like when marketing to consumers, it's a question of value. In order for an Influencer to want to be working with you, they must first perceive that it is advantageous for *them*. If they're doing you a favor by working with you, it's not a business relationship at all, it's a charity.

So how can you go about demonstrating that a business relationship with your Instagram will be advantageous? The easiest way to go about it would be to simply sponsor them. Provide them with free products, share sneak previews, even invite them to check out your business and see what goes on behind the scenes. Establish a relationship with them that provides them with enough value to motivate them to reciprocate.

Working with an Influencer takes time to figure out. You'll need to find an influencer who is popular and active within your customer persona's community. You'll need to determine what your budget is with them and then you will need to do the legwork to reach out to them.

Chances are, if they are extremely popular, they might have very generous offers already, so be prepared for negotiations. But, if you are able to sponsor an influencer, or at the very least, get them to review or promote your products, not only will you be advertising to an extremely relevant target market, you'll also be drawing them towards your own Instagram profile!

However, it is important to note that if you are going to be sponsoring an Influencer, you will need to take the proper steps to make sure people know that the Influencer is being compensated or paid to endorse specific products. This is because the FTC requires that Influencers follow a specific set of guidelines, so that consumers are aware of the compensation. This is known as disclosure and is an ethical thing to do. There's nothing wrong with sponsoring or being paid to review a product, but it is immoral to conceal the fact that they were taking money for doing so. The consumer has a right to know whether an endorsement came organically or if a deal was made.

Taking Bad Photos

The sheer fact that Instagram has become so popular has led to an arms race of sorts when it comes to photo quality. Most companies with Instagram accounts are focused not only on creating quality content but taking high quality pictures as well. This raises the bar for anyone else who wants to be popular on Instagram. As vain as it might sound, people want to see pretty pictures, its why they come to Instagram in the first place.

There is no place for badly shot or poorly lit photographs on Instagram. While there's nothing wrong with the raw, honest types of photos that we get from Instagram Stories, the rest of the posts need to look great. And the best way to achieve this is to get a camera that is of decent quality. You don't have to spend a fortune on a camera, but you should at least try and get one that you can use for dedicated Instagram pictures. The better the photo quality that you use, the more people will enjoy what you are posting.

And besides, when it comes down to it, you're going to need a good camera for the purpose of taking product shots. You don't want to just take pictures of products with phone. While it is true that most phones take fairly decent quality, nothing can replace a good camera. If you're serious about using Instagram as your primary vehicle for marketing, then it's worth the expense.

Forgetting to Reply

We can all be busy, but unfortunately, customers don't have the level of patience that they used to. The fact is, we live in a culture of instant gratification. If a person wants to buy something online, they can get it the next day and, in some cases, the same day! We have the ability to access what we want, when we want and that has created an unfortunate side effect of impatience. People who don't get instant gratification might even end up feeling frustrated or ignored.

This environment and expectation can lead to trouble with customers if they feel that you aren't replying fast enough. In general, you'll want to reply to any concerns or queries sent by your customers within a day, two at the most. This is prompt enough to show them that you care and are actively ready to assist them whenever they need.

However, sometimes you may end up reading a message and then saying, "I'll reply later," only never to do so. This can be frustrating for the consumer, especially if they end up having to wait more than a few days for a reply. Or worse yet, you may have completely forgotten them and never reply to their message in the first place!

This is understandable, but from a business perspective will only cost you both money and goodwill. The best way to prevent this from happening is to adopt a simple policy. If you read it, reply to it. Even if your reply is that you'll get back to them with more information, this will at least help the customer feel acknowledged. Saying that you'll read it later only delays the response and most of the time, questions can be answered fairly quickly.

Using Bots

There are some unethical, shady practices done within in the Instagram community, either by businesses looking to get ahead, or sold by companies looking to make some money off earnest business owners who don't know any better. We already covered one unethical practice, buying followers, but now let's talk about another one: using bots.

A bot is an automated program that performs specific tasks without any need for input from the creator. Bots are often used online as a means of collecting data, filling out forms and performing other tasks. A bot by itself is morally neutral, as it's just a program meant to do as its told. However, there are people online who have decided to create bots that are able to mimic human interaction on Instagram.

These automated bots are able to sift through content, using a type of machine learning similar to what Instagram's algorithms use, in order to find relevant content. The bots can like posts, leave comments and even follow other users. In other words, an Instagram bot can literally do all of the tasks that a human can do, although with varying results due to the fact it is just an artificial intelligence unit.

However, according to Instagram's terms of services, modifying the API in any way is against the rules. And bots do just that, they modify the way Instagram works, outside of Instagram's control. This creates potential for all sorts of security risks and other problems. Using an automated bot for Instagram can lead to a permanent ban of your account.

But there are still companies out there who are willing to offer and sell these bots to the general public. They'll customize them to your specifications and then allow you to use them in exchange for a fee. Sometimes they'll even claim that their work is above board and completely within the rules of Instagram. However, it is important always to check Instagram's terms of service to see if this is actually true.

While it is possible for a bot to boost the results your company will see, by doing the majority of the legwork, there is a large chance you'll get caught by Instagram. Their algorithms have gotten better and better and this type of behavior is well on their radar. If they catch someone using a bot, they will shut the account down entirely. This will more or less destroy all of the hard work done on your business. You will always be hanging by a thread, hoping that somehow Instagram doesn't notice your bot's behavior.

In the end, while it isn't as advantageous to play within the confines of the rules provided, it is much safer. You might not gain all of the benefits of using a fully automated helper to run your IG page, but at the same time, you don't have to worry about suddenly losing all of your hard work.

Does this mean that all types of automation are against the rules? No, not at all. There are certain types of automation that are perfectly acceptable to use, but these things will always plug into Instagram through the proper channels, requiring that you grant them permission to connect your Instagram account.

Tuning Out the News

A lot of things are happening in 2019 when it comes to discussions of advertising, data collection and online privacy. As companies like Facebook and Google continue to grow and become monoliths in their respective fields, people are beginning to wonder if the size of these companies is not growing into monopolies. Meanwhile, the outcry over privacy has led many advocacy groups to condemn the practices that Facebook uses for data collection.

2019 is going to be a turning point in how people view data collection in the United States. Congress is going to be getting involved at some point, potentially with anti-trust actions that could curtail the growth of these two companies. If it gets really bad, these two corporations may end up being broken up by the government.

Of course, this isn't meant to alarm you. There are a lot of changes happening and we are exploring brand new, unfamiliar territory due to the nature of technology being so new. We didn't have social media to this degree 10 years ago. As a result, everything happening is a consequence of a brand new world, where the rules are being made up as we go along. There will naturally be growing pains.

Those who aren't in the loop are the ones who will suffer. Ignoring what is happening in the news, not bothering to stay abreast of current technological disputes and not paying attention can cause you problems in the long run. The internet moves quick and platforms can change in an instant.

Those, however, who are able to pay attention to the trends and watch how the government handles these cases will be in a good position, since they will be able to act proactively. Rather than being in a position where things are suddenly changing for the worse, the savvy marketer will be well aware of what is coming down the pipeline and adjusts to it ahead of time.

In many cases, those who are able to anticipate change and adapt to it quickly are the ones who make it to the top. Those who ignore or don't bother to pay attention to these changes can end up going under entirely.

This talk may seem alarming at first, but rest assured, this is the nature of working in online marketing. What works today might not work tomorrow. There is no guarantee. Even if it weren't the government to cause problems for your preferred social media platform, what would you do if a new platform was released that took 90% of your userbase? If you want to be truly successful in online marketing, you have to be prepared and ready to adapt. Many sudden changes weren't actually as sudden as most people think. They were simply unprepared for what was telegraphed ahead of time.

You may be wondering if perhaps with all these talks about the future of Facebook if it's worth investing the time and energy in learning how to use Instagram. After all, if the government comes at them, all is lost, right? Well, not exactly. First off, things move slowly at a governmental level. It won't be a sudden, swift decision. It will most likely be a few years before any kind of serious action happens at all. Second, the apps themselves aren't in danger. While there will be plenty of policies that do change if the government gets its way, the fact is, people aren't using Instagram for anything other than the fact that they like the app. It has become a way of life for many people. If something were to happen to Facebook, as unlikely as it is, the app itself will probably just be sold and continue to function as is.

As long as you keep an ear to the ground and an eye on Washington, you'll absolutely be able to take full advantage of all that Instagram has to offer. If changes start coming down the pipeline, you'll be in a position to pivot. Don't stay out of the water just because you're worried it might change temperature, because even if it does, there are always different pools to jump in!

Summary

Instagram is showing no signs of slowing down when it comes to both growth and innovation. Hashtags are just as relevant as ever and most people prefer to use upwards to 30 of them per post.

Instagram TV is brand new to the scene and does have some promise, although it is uncertain whether or not it will be a success. Large brands in the past have failed at major endeavors like IGTV and competing with YouTube is no small task. Still, the link between IGTV and Instagram is advantageous for those who are looking to branch into long form video.

There are a wide variety of tools out there that allow you to make the most of Instagram. Some of them are free, while others do have monthly subscription costs. There is nothing wrong with using a few tools to help you get a competitive edge, provided that these tools are approved for use by Instagram. While there are other shortcuts through unethical territory, those shortcuts will only lead to problems for you down the road.

Instagram Influencers are continuing to grow as a major marketing force in 2019. It would be a tremendous mistake to ignore them, but it would also be a mistake to try and get them to help you out as a favor to you. Reaching out to them, establishing a professional business relationship and working to provide as much value to the Influencer as possible will bring plenty of rewards your way. It may end up being expensive, but the costs are well worth it, especially if the Influencer has an active following of your exact customer persona.

Chapter 8: Getting Ahead

In this chapter, we're going to be focusing on the various ways that you can get ahead in your Instagram endeavors. We'll be sharing tips, tricks and popular methods of developing a comprehensive content plan and minimizing the time you spend while maximizing the results.

Keep an Eye on the Competition

When it comes to getting ahead in the world of Instagram, you don't have to reinvent the wheel. There are already plenty of successful businesses out there who are using Instagram to get tremendous results. Fortunately, the nature of social media means that their work is entirely public, you can just go to any business's profile that you wish and see exactly how they are posting. You can watch their content strategy, see how they interact with others and more importantly, learn from them.

You should always be willing to keep an eye on your competition, as well as the larger companies, to determine if there is any way to emulate them. There's nothing wrong with copying a competitor, especially if that competitor is successful in their endeavors. Of course, there is a caveat to this. You should be willing to copy the successful strategies that your competitors are using, but you shouldn't be willing to take their photos and content and use them for your own. And you should also make a point to avoid plagiarizing their ideas for content as well. You want to keep your brand identity interesting and diverse. So, feel free to take their strategies, but make sure that you develop your own content.

Another benefit behind keeping an eye on your competition is that you'll be able to get a pulse for how they are developing as a company. Are they charging more or less for similar products? Are they getting major buzz when they release a new Instagram story? You can also look at customer comments and reactions to try and gauge how consumers feel about their products. Perhaps you might even be able to glean a weakness, some kind of shortcoming that the customers are dissatisfied with. This can give you ideas of *how* to market your own products, perhaps even addressing the shortcomings of your competitors, without having to mention them.

Developing A Content Calendar

The biggest challenge that most business face when they first get started with Instagram is figuring out what kind of content they want to create. Worse yet, it can be troublesome having to sit down each day, thinking of what to post. Over time, it can grow exhausting and even frustrating. Fortunately, there are ways to prevent this type of fatigue and burnout from affecting you.

The easiest way to plan out your content is to use a content calendar. A content calendar is just a template with days and months, helping you sort out your ideas and plan what you want to create and release in the future. By sitting down and planning all of the content that you intend to make at once, you will be freeing up your mind to simply work according to the calendar. The more decisions that you cut out in the future, the easier it is to sit down and focus on the task at hand.

The first step to making a content calendar is to list out the different types of content that you want to release. For example, you could list infographics, behind the scenes and product photos as what you want to release during Week 1. After you determine which content you want to release for the first week, you then select which days you will be releasing each type of that content. So, you could determine to release an Infographic on Monday, Behind the Scenes on Wednesday and Friday, and Product photos on Saturday. You list these plans out on those specific days on the calendar.

Then, from there, you just fill in the entire month with the appropriate content that you wish to release. It's good to have a monthly plan for a content calendar, but it's not a great idea to go past a month. Why? Because you'll need to analyze the metrics to see how all of your content has done at the end of the month. You don't want to schedule too far out ahead, or else you may end up having committed to a content strategy that simply isn't working. Taking it a month at a time will help you refine your process and eventually develop razor sharp content that delivers every time!

Scheduling Out

After you have developed your content calendar, the next, bigger task will be going about creating all of the necessary content to release over the course of the next month. But the good news is that if you're going to use a content scheduler like Buffer, you will be able to do all of the scheduling in one sitting. After the content has been made, all you need to do is dedicate a day to follow your calendar, scheduling each specific post to a day and a time. Then, you're good to go for the month! All you need to worry about at that point is replying to your followers, making comments on others posts and creating your own Instagram stories, which can't be scheduled in advanced.

You will find that this process of planning everything ahead of time and allowing the scheduling program to handle the rest will greatly cut down on the amount of active time you use Instagram. And the best part is, even though you are doing considerably less work, you are still going to be getting all of the results of a regular poster! Even more so, when you consider that sometimes people end up forgetting to post, or end up too busy due to business opportunities in the daytime.

The assembly line style of creating a calendar first, then content, then scheduling, will reduce the sheer number of time and effort that you will need to spend. But it does have a downside. Some of the work can be a little tedious, especially when it comes to creating posts ahead of time. However, it is a discipline worth developing, because soon you won't have to be worrying about whether or not you posted today. You get all of the rewards of being a regular poster, but with none of the drawbacks.

Managing Responses

Another reason you should be using a central content planner such as Buffer, is that you will also have the ability to respond to direct messages or even comments from the website. This means that if you're dealing with a significant influx of people commenting or asking questions, you won't have to sort through them all using Instagram itself. Rather than sorting through and tapping out individual responses on your phone, you can simply use your computer to sort and then type replies, which is considerably faster than doing it all on your phone.

Create Teams

As a small business, you may not have a lot of employees working for you, but if you do have others involved in the business, you might want to consider creating team profiles. These profiles allow for others to create posts, edit or reply to your Instagram posts, all while using a social media manager. This can help divide the workload. Best of all, you can assign different permissions, depending on what role you want your team members to play. Some might be able to post, while others may only be allowed to reply.

Hire a Virtual Assistant

Creating content can be time consuming and difficult, especially if you haven't done it before. Rather than simply go it alone, spending all of your time creating content, you may want to consider hiring a virtual assistant. Thanks to the power of online connectivity, more and more people are looking to find work online. Known as virtual assistants, these people can be hired to assist you in your online work, doing a wide variety of tasks in exchange for pay.

There are upsides and downsides to using a virtual assistant. Let's focus on the upsides first. Expertise is the biggest value that you get when it comes to hiring a virtual assistant. Thanks to the dozens of websites out there that let you find and hire the right kind of people, you can be assured that you will be hiring someone who clearly understands what you are looking for. If you want someone to create content, you will have a wide pool of experts who are able to sit down and put together great looking photos for your business.

Another upside to using a virtual assistant is that you are freeing up a major chunk of your time. By outsourcing these tasks, you are able to focus your efforts elsewhere on the business. You can do what you do best, while also getting good results from your assistant. It's a win-win situation.

Since hiring a virtual assistant is a contracting job, you also don't have to worry about paperwork or signing them on as an employee. These are work for hire positions that can be easily terminated if the employee isn't working out. You don't have to worry about being stuck with someone who isn't willing to do the hard work. If they are underperforming, you can just as easily find a new virtual assistant who is willing to do what needs to be done.

There are downsides, of course, to hiring a virtual assistant. There is the price factor. Most of the time, you're going to be paying them an hourly wage, which can stack up, especially if you have a lot of work for them. However, working with a virtual assistant is significantly cheaper than just deciding to go with a Social Media Marketing Agency, who often charges an arm and leg for services you could do yourself.

Another downside is that you'll primarily be working with a freelancer who might not have the same schedule as you. While they will still get the work done, they won't be available to talk immediately, especially if they aren't in the same time zone. This can lead to a message tag, so if you're expecting immediate replies during your normal hours, you may end up disappointed.

One thing you won't have to worry about too much is security risks. You can create team profiles for your virtual assistant, so they only have limited access to your accounts and they won't have administrative rights to do anything permanent. On top of that, most of the agencies or platforms that allow you to hire virtual assistances have ratings. You will be able to see the ratings that a specific virtual assistant has, how much they've worked and how many clients they've worked with. This should help to give you a picture of the employees' general skillset and how well they get along with their clients. Most importantly, you won't have to worry about hiring someone untrustworthy or unethical. If they have strong social proof and a high rating, you're in good hands.

Ultimately, a virtual assistant can supercharge your Instagram efforts, especially if you are limited on time. And, best of all, if they are truly good at what they do, they will ultimately end up generating you more money in the future, as their work will help bring in new followers and product sales.

Summary

Your time is extremely valuable and should be treated as such. Rather than treat Instagram Marketing as if it were a daily chore, it would be far better to plan everything out in advanced.

Creating a content calendar will help you have the proper direction for when you create content. It will give you focus and reduce the amount of time you need to think about things other than content creation. This creates an assembly-line effect, where you aren't losing energy going back and forth from one topic to the other. Rather, you are able to stay focused on each part of the content equation until you are finished.

A social media managing program is necessary if you wish to take Instagram Marketing seriously. Scheduling posts well ahead of time frees you up entirely, so that you are able to focus on other things during your business day. You won't have to worry about forgetting to post every day and most importantly, you will be free to focus on the things that matter: responding and replying to comments.

You don't have to manage everything by yourself, rather you can opt to create a team with the help of a social media managing program, putting other members of your staff in charge, all the while restricting access to admin rights, so they don't end up causing trouble. If you don't have the staff for such a task, you can also outsource a virtual assistant who will act as a dedicated assistant, well versed in picking up the slack where it is necessary. Whether you're looking for someone to handle customer service, create content or just simply develop the content calendar, a virtual assistant is well worth the money.

Chapter 9: Conclusion

As we come to the end of this book, it is our hope that you have learned a great deal about what makes for a successful Instagram marketer. Let's review a few of the major concepts presented here:

It's All About Them

Ultimately, a customer only cares about what they perceive to be valuable. You can have the best product in the world, but until you take the time to learn what speaks to your customer, you won't be able to market it to them. If you focus overwhelmingly about your customers and followers, learning what they value and providing them with content that lifts them up, you will be very successful in building a following.

Consequently, if you only talk about yourself and your own products, regardless of how great they are, you will end up being ignored. No one wants to have a conversation with a narcissist, both in the real world and online. Keep the sales talk to a minimum. Remember, nobody cares about what you know until they know that you care.

Engaging With Followers is Necessary

You can't just expect to rack up a large number of followers and then watch as the sales come flowing in. You'll need to cultivate real, honest relationships with these followers in order to gain their trust. Once they become familiar with you and trust you, it will be easier to show them the products that will help improve their lives. But without engagement, they won't know that you are honest and earnest with them.

Focus Beyond the Sale

A sale is a single transaction that happens once and then it's over. While sales are necessary for the lifeblood of your company, you're going to need more than just sales if you want to really thrive. You're going to want to turn your followers into advocates who are raving fans. This takes time and intentionality to pull off. You must be able to develop strategies that tell your company story to your followers while also bolstering their loyalty.

Contests, giveaways and discounts for those who follow you closely are some of the best ways to reward them for their loyalty. Responding to their questions quickly and being honest when they are unhappy with your service will go incredibly far in helping fans turn into superfans.

Paid Advertising Is Important

Organic use of Instagram will aid you in maintaining the relationships and connections that you have made, but without paid advertising, your company will inch along. You can pick up the pace and save a lot of time by using the powerful advertising system that Instagram provides, either through doing traditional scrolling ads or story ads.

You simply cannot neglect to use the paid advertising system when it comes to Instagram. You will make significantly more sales than if you were to solely rely on organic reach. Both are important, of course, but in different respects. You have to spend money to make money, this principle never changes, no matter the business.

Always Be Learning:

When it comes to online platforms and social media, things are in a constant state of flux. We've done as best we can to provide a snapshot of what the current climate is for Instagram in 2019, but like all things online, the picture will soon change. Pay attention to what the trends are, look for what the news is saying about the future of Instagram and never stop learning. The more you learn, the better poised you are to not only adapt to sudden changes, but also to thrive in the online marketplace.

Instagram is a powerful tool for marketing, but it's not the only one that exists online. Indeed, we've touched a lot on Facebook's advertising system, mainly because they are closely tied to Instagram due to being owned and operated by the same company. If you're interested in learning more about how you can incorporate Facebook into your overall marketing, check out *Facebook Marketing and Advertising for Small Business Owners in 2019*. Inside, you'll find all the necessary things for creating a proper Facebook page, how to use Facebook Business Manager and how to take full advantage of what Facebook advertising has to offer.

Or, if you're looking to develop a more focused way to convert customers, taking them from a cold state and warming them up enough to make a purchase and more, you should read *Sales Funnel Management For Small Business Owners in 2019*. Both of these books will provide you will all of the principles and ideas necessary to make money online, all the while building up a customer base that is crazy about you!

That's all that we have for you. We sincerely hope that you are able to get the most out of this guide and that you are successful in building the best Instagram profile possible. Good luck!

Dear reader,

As

   an independent author, and one man/woman operation - my marketing budget is next to zero.

As such, the

   only

   way I can get my books in-front of valued customers if with reviews.

Unfortunately,
   I'm competing against authors and giant publishing companies with multi-million dollar marketing teams. These behemoths can afford to give away hundreds of free books to boost their ranking and success. Which as much as I'd love to - I simply can't afford to do.

That's
   why your honest review will not only be invaluable to me, but also to other readers on Amazon.

Best wishes,

Mark Warner

Further reading

Facebook still has the biggest user base. Moreover, it has been accepted among all each groups, while Instagram´s reach focusses on the younger people.

Because Facebook in 2019 still has the biggest reach, don´t miss out on revenue with Facebook with the following resource.

https://amzn.to/301yHZF

Title
Facebook Marketing and Advertising for Small Business Owners in 2019

Subtitle
Discover How to Optimize the Money You Spend on Facebook And Get Maximum Results By Using Proven ROI Methods

Here is a tiny bit of what you´ll discover:

- The Ad-types and targeting used by a now famous Korean Fashion Brand **to get a 15 times ROI using Facebook Ads** (page 38)
- The 9 core principles to power Your Facebook Strategy (page 12)
- A practical 8 step checklist to setup and manage your Facebook Ads, **miss 1 and your Facebook Ad will fail** (page 18)
- 6 Tips to create Engaging Content for higher conversion rates, miss a few tips and you are throwing away money (page 28)
- **The Facebook strategies used by a famous car brand to make their model the no. 1 in the segment and how you can leverage their tactics** (page 40)
- 12 Tools which will help to push your Facebook Marketing results to the next level (page 30)
- 17 Mind blowing facts and numbers about Facebook platform, **which you can use for your strategic Facebook Marketing Planning** (page 34)

- 6 Things people are looking for on Facebook, use this to choose the right type of Ad (page 35)
- **Step-by-step guide to create your ideal customer persona for maximum profits, including practical examples** (page 49)
- More than 60 Facebook Marketing Tips for Small Businesses which still pay-off (page 71)
- How to make a post that goes viral, backed by numbers and customer psychology (page 94)
- **Why, when and how you should setup Facebook Pixels for better ROI** (page 102)
- 3 Tips for engaging storytelling through Facebook to further increase the loyalty of your customers for your brand (page 138)
- **5 Tips to prevent wasting time and money on Facebook** (page 121)

And much, much more.

Don´t waste more time and learn the tricks leveraged by other successful small companies.

https://amzn.to/301yHZF

Audiobook version

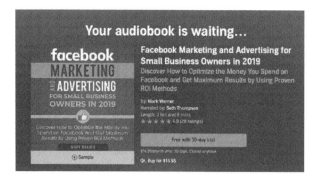

If you feel like you don´t have enough time to read about Facebook Marketing in 2019 for Small Business Owners, I have great news. You can listen to the **audio version** of this book for **FREE**, by signing up for FREE for the 30-day audible trail.

You can cancel the trial any time for any reason.

Audible Trial Benefits:

- **FREE audio copy** of this book

- After, the free trail, you will get 1 credit per month to use on any audiobook available.

- Choose from Audible´s 200,000 + titles

- Listen anywhere with the Audible app across multiple devices

- If you don´t love an audiobook, exchange easy for another one without hassle

- You will keep your audiobooks forever, even if your cancel your membership

And much, much more

Click on one of the below links and start listening for FREE to this $14,95 audiobook.

Link to FREE audiobook US: https://adbl.co/2JhSgWN
Link to FREE audiobook UK: https://adbl.co/2YtRXyq
Link to FREE audiobook France: http://bit.ly/31XkLl4
Link to FREE audiobook Germany: https://adbl.co/2YrZM7U

Printed in Great Britain
by Amazon